Wesleyan Missions:
Their Progress Stated and
Their Claims Enforced

by

Robert Alder

First Fruits Press
Wilmore, Kentucky
c2016

Wesleyan Missions: their progress stated and their claims enforced.
By Robert Alder

First Fruits Press, © 2016
Previously published by the Wesleyan Missionary Society, 1842.

ISBN: 9781621714545 (print), 9781621714606 (digital), 9781621714613 (kindle)

Digital version at http://place.asburyseminary.edu/firstfruitsbooks/9/

Alder, Robert.

Wesleyan missions: their progress stated and their claims enforced./ by Robert Alder.
vii, 104 pages ; 21 cm.
Wilmore, Kentucky : First Fruits Press, ©2016.
Reprint. Previously published: London : Wesleyan Missionary Society, 1842.
ISBN: 9781621714545 (pbk.)

1. Wesleyan Methodist Church--Missions. 2. Wesleyan Methodist Missionary Society. I. Title.

BV2550.A8 2015

Cover design by Jonathan Ramsay

asburyseminary.edu
800.2ASBURY
204 North Lexington Avenue
Wilmore, Kentucky 40390

First Fruits
THE ACADEMIC OPEN PRESS OF ASBURY SEMINARY

First Fruits Press
The Academic Open Press of Asbury Theological Seminary
204 N. Lexington Ave., Wilmore, KY 40390
859-858-2236
first.fruits@asburyseminary.edu
asbury.to/firstfruits

WESLEYAN MISSIONS:

THEIR PROGRESS STATED AND THEIR CLAIMS ENFORCED.

WITH OBSERVATIONS AND SUGGESTIONS

APPLICABLE TO

KINDRED INSTITUTIONS.

BY ROBERT ALDER, D.D.,

ONE OF THE GENERAL SECRETARIES OF THE WESLEYAN
MISSIONARY SOCIETY.

" Is there not a cause ? "

FOURTEENTH THOUSAND.

LONDON:

PUBLISHED BY THE WESLEYAN MISSIONARY SOCIETY,

CENTENARY-HALL, BISHOPSGATE:

SOLD ALSO BY JOHN MASON, 66, PATERNOSTER-ROW;
AND J. NISBETT, BERNERS'-STREET.

1842.

LONDON:

PRINTED BY JAMES NICHOLS,

HOXTON-SQUARE.

TO

THE REVEREND JABEZ BUNTING, D.D.,

PRESIDENT OF THE WESLEYAN THEOLOGICAL INSTITUTION

&c., &c.

WHOSE NAME IS IDENTIFIED

WITH WESLEYAN METHODISM,

AND

WHOSE CHARACTER, INFLUENCE, AND COUNSELS

HAVE SO EMINENTLY CONTRIBUTED TO EXTEND AND CONSOLIDATE

THE WESLEYAN MISSIONS

IN EVERY QUARTER OF THE GLOBE,

THE FOLLOWING PAGES ARE INSCRIBED,

WITH SENTIMENTS OF MUCH RESPECT AND ESTEEM,

BY

HIS FAITHFUL FRIEND AND COLLEAGUE,

THE AUTHOR.

PREFACE.

THE following statement of the progress and claims of the Wesleyan Missions owes its existence to an impression which was made on the mind of the Author, while attending a series of Special Missionary Meetings in the West of England, during the month of November last,—that the present Missionary crisis calls for a work of this description. An apology, founded upon the pressure of numerous engagements, and the performance of official duties, is one usually offered for errors and imperfections in literary productions, and might truly and justly be pleaded in this instance. But the Author cannot allow himself to adopt that course, because he feels that he might have postponed this publication, if he had deemed it proper so to do; and that he of set purpose accomplished his task quickly, from a paramount desire to serve a good cause with promptitude. It is due, however, to himself, and a mark of respect to his readers, to add, that, although the work has been rapidly composed, he hopes it is not justly chargeable with hasty inconsideration or thoughtless negligence.

The manuscript was prepared with a particular reference to the existing state and prospects of the Wesleyan Missionary Society; and, in compliance with the request of the General Committee, it is now published, under the auspices and for the benefit of that Institution. But the publication will probably be of service to kindred Societies, by pointing out the real cause of their pecuniary embarrassments, and by showing, that the means which they, as well as the Wesleyan Missionary Society, have employed for the propagation of the Gospel of God our Saviour, have been accompanied and followed by the most cheering results, and afford the best encouragement to enlarged and more vigorous efforts for sending it amongst all nations.

The present age may be regarded as the Missionary era of the church and of the world, and as one in which all who love "the truth as it is in Jesus" are especially called upon strenuously to exert themselves in sowing, as speedily and as extensively as possible, the "incorruptible seed which liveth and abideth for ever." Whatever changes may take place in the social or political state of the nations of the earth; however severe and painful the trials may be through which they may have to pass; whatever may be the immediate results of the great conflict of sentiment and of system which has already commenced, and is waged with so much earnestness and determination of purpose; the seed of the kingdom will "take root downward, and bear fruit upward," which shall be for the healing of the nations. The services which British Christianity is now rendering, in the furtherance of this great object, can never be forgotten. Should it please God to permit England to fall from her present high estate; should this great country cease to be what she now is,—the asylum of freedom, the mart of commerce and of manufactures, the ark of true religion, and the leader of the Missionary hosts of Protestantism; it will be remembered to her honour, by future generations, while partaking of the blessedness of that golden age which the world shall yet witness, and to which the finger of promise and of prophecy point,—that her sons and her daughters nobly contributed to produce the harvest which shall then be reaped with so much joy. As recollections of the glory of ancient Rome are now awakened by the sight of those remains of material splendour and magnificence which are still to be found in the streets and palaces of that city, once the mistress of the world, so the improved moral aspects which, by means of the present Missionary efforts of England, many nations may in future times present, will furnish a memorial to the honour of our country, more durable and more precious than any which human skill or power is capable of forming from Italian marble, or Corinthian brass.

ROBERT ALDER.

HATTON-GARDEN, LONDON,
  Feb. 21*st*, 1842.

WESLEYAN MISSIONS:

&c., &c.

I.

It pleases God, who worketh all things after the counsel of his own will, for the accomplishment of events designed to exercise an extensive and permanent bearing upon the welfare of men, to use means that to merely human wisdom appear to be inadequate to secure the ends for which they are employed; and then, contrary to all human expectation, to crown, with the most signal success, the simple agencies which he selects:—a truth, of which the annals of Wesleyan Methodism furnish numerous and striking proofs and illustrations.

In an Assembly,—composed of Preachers of the Gospel, who were raised up by the providence and grace of God, during an extraordinary period, for the accomplishment of an extraordinary work,—held in the year 1769, in the town of Leeds, a place of renown in the records of Methodism, the Venerable Wesley, who presided on that occasion, inquired, "Who will go to help our brethren in America?" Two of his "sons in the Gospel" responded to the call, and willingly offered themselves for this "work of faith, and labour of love." A collection was then made by those evangelical successors of the Apostles, which amounted to fifty pounds. A portion of the money thus raised was expended in defraying the expenses connected with the passage of the two Missionaries across the Atlantic; and the remainder was sent, in the true spirit of Christian charity, "as a proof of brotherly love," to assist the Trustees of a Chapel in John-Street, New-York, —at that period, the only one in America belonging to the Wesleyan Methodists,—in defraying the expenses incurred in its erection. Thus may be said to have commenced the foreign operations of the "Conference of the

B

Ministers in the Connexion established by the late Rev. John Wesley, A.M.,"—at the suggestion, and under the direction, of that distinguished Servant of God himself.

This movement attracted little or no attention, either on the part of the Church or of the world ; and yet it has already produced consequences of surpassing interest and magnitude. Although scarcely more than " threescore years and ten" have since then passed away, revolutions, rapid and violent as the whirlwind, have, during that time, visited both hemispheres, and have effected stupendous changes in the political state and relations of each ; but, during the whole of this eventful period, while the very foundations of the earth were shaken, the evangelical leaven, which was carried to America by Joseph Pilmoor and Richard Boardman, two humble and faithful men, has been silently, but effectually, operating upon vast masses of the inhabitants of the United States ; many of whom, though they have embraced the principles contained in Paine's " Rights of Man," on questions connected with Civil Government, have yet been prevented from adopting, in reference to the all-important subject of religion, the principles embodied in his " Age of Reason," —a circumstance for which they are in no small degree indebted to the effects which have been produced by the introduction amongst them of the doctrines and discipline of Methodism. That Church, the foundations of which were thus unostentatiously and prayerfully laid, has been, and still is, Missionary in her character, as well as in her origin ; and she now numbers her Pastors by thousands, and includes within her pale a greater number of members, and " hearers of the word," than is to be found connected with any other form of Christianity in the Republic.*

The second important Missionary movement, on the part of the Wesleyan Community, is also associated with the American Continent ; but it led to a field of labour and usefulness very different from that which was originally contemplated, and one in which Methodism has gained some of its noblest triumphs. This enterprise

* See Note A at the end of the volume.

was intrusted by Mr. Wesley to Dr. Coke, whose heart was intent on the salvation of the world;—who never shrank from any duty, however painful or humiliating, in which the interests of Christian Missions were involved; —whose memory is consecrated by his zeal, labours, and sacrifices on their behalf;—and whose very death was over-ruled, by the wisdom and goodness of the Great Head of the Church, to the extension of the good cause which he so eminently promoted during his life. That excellent man left England in the year 1786, accompanied by three Missionaries, bound for Nova-Scotia. But the vessel was forced, by stress of weather, to proceed to the Island of Antigua; by which providential arrangement, that gracious work of God commenced in the West Indies, which, viewed under the various aspects that it presents, has, perhaps, not been surpassed since the first ages of Christianity.

The agents of other denominations have, at subsequent periods, entered into the same field, more especially since the abolition of slavery; but it should not be forgotten, that, for many years, the Moravian and Wesleyan Missionaries were, with a very few exceptions, the only religious instructors of the servile population of that portion of the empire. During the reign of slavery, they chiefly bore the burden and heat of the day; and, by the blessing of God on their self-denying services, mainly contributed to prepare the way for the state of universal freedom and religious tranquillity which now exists in those Colonies, as well as to produce the favourable change which has taken place in the opinions of the planters generally, concerning the character and tendency of Christian Missions.

II.

THE Missionary efforts of the Connexion have been greatly extended since the period which has been just noticed. A branch, which the great tree of evangelical Truth began to put forth only a hundred years ago, is already spreading into all lands, and is laden with the gracious fruits of righteousness, charity, and peace. If those to whose care it is committed continue faithful to the trust reposed in them, it will " be to the Lord for a name, and for an everlasting sign that shall not be cut off." In addition to the places previously occupied in America and the West Indies, Missionary operations were commenced on the Continent of Europe, as early as the year 1791; on the African Continent, in 1811; and in Asia, during the year 1814. Australasia was first visited by a Wesleyan Missionary in the course of the following year; and Polynesia, where the word of the Lord has been so eminently glorified, in 1822. It will be seen from this statement, that the field in which the labourers belonging to this Society are employed, is emphatically and pre-eminently THE WORLD. On the shores of Sweden, and in the Upper Alps;—at Gibraltar and Malta; —on the banks of the Gambia, at Sierra Leone, and on the Gold Coast;—at "the Cape of Storms;"—in Ceylon, and on the shores of Southern India;—amongst the Colonists and Aboriginal tribes of Australia, in New-Zealand, the Friendly Islands, and Feejee;—on the islands of the Western, as well as of the Southern, Hemisphere;—and from the Gulf of St. Lawrence to the far West;—the Agents of the Wesleyan Missionary Society are found. To all these places,—to a portion of the people by whom they are inhabited,—to man in all those regions,—the British Conference has sent the Gospel of our salvation, since the question was asked, in 1769, " Who will go to help our brethren in America?"

III.

THE Wesleyan Missionary Society has arrived at such a crisis in its affairs, that it must EITHER EXTEND, OR CONTRACT, THE SPHERE OF ITS OPERATIONS. That noble Institution must ere long be placed in such circumstances as will enable it adequately to maintain and strengthen the Stations which it occupies, and the Agents whom it employs. Unless this is done, and done speedily and effectually too, we may expect soon to hear of the operations of one or more of those Missionary presses being suspended, which are now providing the means of spiritual instruction and mental improvement for reclaimed Heathens and Barbarians;—of the closing of Missionary

Schools and Chapels, in which multitudes of adults and children are taught how they may obtain wisdom, pardon, holiness, and heaven ; " knowledge, which cannot be gotten for gold, nor shall silver be weighed for the price thereof;"—of Missionary Churches being deprived of adequate pastoral care ;—and of some of those spots, which, by labours and prayers, and gifts and sacrifices, had been recovered from the wilderness of Heathenism, being abandoned to their former sad and cheerless condition. It cannot be too distinctly or too frequently repeated, that, if the present pecuniary difficulties which embarrass the movements of that great Missionary machine which the Wesleyan section of the Christian Church has set and hitherto kept in motion, are not removed by the efforts of those from whom it ought to receive its needful and continued *momentum*, the progress of human improvement and salvation, by the instrumentality of scriptural truth, will in some places be greatly retarded, and in others, for a season at least, be entirely prevented.

The Wesleyan Society is not the only Missionary Institution of the present day which has to grapple with pecuniary difficulties. This cause of embarrassment is felt, in at least an equal degree, by every section of the Protestant Church, whose Ministers and members are actively engaged in the sublime enterprise, which has for its object the diffusion of evangelical truth and righteousness throughout the world. WITH ONE VOICE, THEY COMPLAIN OF THE INADEQUACY OF THEIR RESOURCES, AS COMPARED WITH THE EXTENT OF THEIR ENGAGEMENTS, AND WITH THE URGENT CLAIMS WHICH ARE MADE UPON THEM FROM UNVISITED PORTIONS OF THE GLOBE.

IV.

WHEN, upon a certain occasion, some of the Pharisees and Sadducees tempted the Saviour, " desiring a sign from heaven," He answered and said unto them, " When it is evening, ye say, It will be fair weather, for the sky is red. And in the morning, It will be foul weather to-day, for the sky is red and lowering. O ye hypocrites, ye can discern the face of the sky ; but can ye not discern the signs of the times?" At another time, while addressing an innumerable multitude of people, he said unto them, " When ye see a cloud rise out of the west, straightway ye say, There cometh a shower; and so it is. And when ye see the south wind blow, ye say, There will be heat; and it cometh to pass. Ye hypocrites, ye can discern the face of the sky and of the earth; but how is it that ye do not discern this time?" An important principle is involved in the admonitory language employed by our Lord on these occasions, which may be extensively applied. In this respect, God " has not left himself without witness," in the material creation; for he has so arranged every part of this great system, that certain atmospheric appearances and operations are made so palpably to indicate approaching changes in the state of the weather, that even the beasts of the field, and the fowls of the air, as well as human beings, are warned by them of approaching danger, and are led to make provision for their defence and security. Surely, then, we may reasonably suppose, that those great movements and changes which, at certain periods, take place in the moral world, will be preceded by such premonitory intimations that God is coming forth from his " holy temple," as can neither be overlooked nor misunderstood by the attentive inquirer, who believes that the Lord " ruleth over all the kingdoms of men." To attempt to pry into " the times and the seasons," which the Father hath kept in his own power, or to presume to remove any portion of the covering which he has been pleased to spread over his purposes and ways, would argue great rashness and folly. It is, however, by no means inconsistent with that humble and patient frame and temper of mind which the Gospel enjoins,—nay, it is an important part of Christian duty,— to " search and inquire diligently" into the counsels and designs of the Godhead, as they are shadowed forth to us by the movements of Providence, in connexion with the varying phases which the social and religious state of the human family exhibits, or by means of the light which is shed upon them by the oracles of truth.

The present age is deeply and strongly marked by a combination of events, the influence of which is felt and acknowledged in the cabinets of Princes and in the schools of science, as well as in the sanctuaries of religion. Different individuals do, indeed, entertain various opinions as to the cause or causes of those political and moral aspects which the world presents; but their existence is denied by none: and no presumption can justly be attached to the prediction, that future historians will have to describe the period upon which the entire human family is now entering, as one of those great eras in the history of the species which are always marked by extensive changes in the state of individual and collective man. In this respect, the age in which we live may well be compared to the one which gave birth to the Reformation. Those who saw that formidable structure of error, in which, as in a prison, the mind of Christendom had been so long shut up, smitten, as with a thunderbolt, by Luther's appeal from Popes and Councils, to the Word of God, witnessed also the revival of literature; the origin of the art of printing; the discovery of a new world by the indomitable energy and perseverance of one man; masses of human beings arraying themselves against almost every institution, human and divine; and the most potent monarchs of Europe perpetually contending with each other in sanguinary and expensive wars; while the social condition of their respective kingdoms were undergoing important changes, the effects of which are still felt, and will long remain. Such were " the signs of the times" then; and what do we see now? We behold events of a different character, indeed, from those which have been enumerated; but which, nevertheless, are invested with the deepest interest, and entitled to the most profound attention. It will be only needful to refer, in support of this sentiment, to the unexampled influence which is exercised by the press; the discoveries which have been made in the physical sciences, and the degree to which they have been applied to the purposes of commerce and manufactures at home and abroad; the facilities which are afforded for emigration to new regions of the globe; the extent to which colonization is carried; the restlessness and dissatisfaction of large classes of men; the frequency and eagerness with which they investigate and discuss the very first axioms of social order; the desire for change by which they are influenced; the ample manner in which the principle of combination, now so well understood, is actually carried out, for the accomplishment of particular objects; the vast colonial possessions of Great Britain; the movements and changes which are taking place in the East, affording as they do strong reasons to believe that they will be so over-ruled as to lead to changes in the internal state and external relations of the Turkish and Chinese Empires, favourable to the spread of Scriptural Christianity in those countries; the maintenance of amicable relations amongst the great European Powers during the long period which has elapsed since the overthrow of Napoleon, notwithstanding the occurrence of perplexing and irritating events which, but for the intervention of the gracious providence of God, must have terminated in war and bloodshed; the supersedence, in no small degree, of the dominion of superstition in Papal, Mahommedan, and Pagan countries by scepticism; the state of isolation in which different portions of the great Christian family, holding substantially the same views of Scriptural Doctrine, and aiming at the same object, are placed towards each other, and yet, in the midst of much strife and contention, the noble efforts which they are making for the salvation of the Heathen, and the harmonious manner in which they have hitherto conducted their Missionary operations.*

These are some of the striking and peculiar characteristics which present themselves to the view of " the men of this generation," and on which they should seriously meditate; "pondering" them in their hearts, as the

* It is much to be desired that this spirit may continue to be cultivated by the Directors of Missionary Societies, and by Missionaries, towards each other. But in the present divided state of things in the church, it will require no ordinary measure of divine wisdom and charity, to enable them to maintain " the unity of the spirit in the bond of peace." Any attempt to force external uniformity in the forms of religious worship, and in the management of Missions, will issue in strife and confusion.

mother of Jesus did, in reference to the things connected with the birth of the Redeemer. It is recorded to the honour of " the children of Issachar, that they were men that had understanding of the times; to know what Israel ought to do." We live during an eventful age, and should endeavour to understand the times; that, as Christians, we may know what we " ought to do." Amongst all those circumstances which combine to distinguish the present period as one of pre-eminent importance, there is none more deserving our notice, or more likely to engage the attention of Christians, than the fact that, WHILE THERE NEVER WAS A TIME WHEN THE GREAT HEAD OF THE CHURCH VOUCHSAFED TO GRANT MORE SIGNAL AND ENCOURAGING PROOFS OF THE SUCCESS OF PROTESTANT MISSIONARIES ABROAD, THERE NEVER WAS A PERIOD WHEN THE SOCIETIES, UNDER WHOSE DIRECTION THEY ARE EMPLOYED, WERE SO GREATLY EMBARRASSED BY FINANCIAL DIFFICULTIES. In the United States of America, the Missionary Society of the Methodist Episcopal Church, the American Board of Commissioners for Foreign Missions, and other Sections of the Transatlantic Missionary host, have extensive fields open before them, in which glorious triumphs might be gained; and men possessing high intellectual qualifications, deep piety, ardent zeal, and great singleness of purpose, ready to go forth to turn to flight the armies of the aliens. But, alas! the funds of those Societies are exhausted, and their Conductors have not the necessary means for sending the Soldiers of the Cross, who are able and willing to go and " fight the good fight" of faith in heathen lands. On the Continent of Europe, especially in France, in Switzerland, and in the States of Northern Germany, in which the Reformed Faith is professed, the same monetary deficiencies are severely felt, and deeply bewailed, by the faithful few in those countries who cherish the reviving Missionary zeal of our common Protestantism. At Home, a similar state of things exists, and has lately engaged the anxious attention of the Secretaries of the principal Missionary Societies, at more than one of those truly Catholic Meetings which they hold together, at stated periods, for prayer and consultation, and, by means of which, mutual co-operation, without compromise, is so effectually promoted. The very fact that such Meetings are held, strikingly illustrates the uniting tendency of the Missionary spirit and enterprise, and furnishes an instructive lesson to all Missionaries, and to all the friends of Missions. "Behold how good and how pleasant it is for brethren to dwell together in unity!" The excess of Disbursements over the Income of the Church Missionary Society, for the year ending March 31st, 1841, amounted to upwards of £8,000; and it is stated that the Committee, during the present year, have, for the first time, been placed under the necessity of borrowing money, to meet the current expenses of the Society.

Equally discouraging, in a financial point of view, are the circumstances of the London, the Baptist, and the Moravian Missionary Societies; as appears from the latest published Reports of those excellent Institutions, the pages of which furnish ample evidence of the existence of FOREIGN SUCCESS and of DOMESTIC EMBARRASSMENTS.

V.

FROM the preceding statements and observations, it will be seen that the Wesleyan Missionary Society only participates in trials and difficulties which kindred Institutions are now called to endure. This is a mitigating consideration; for, if it were otherwise, fears and apprehensions might be entertained, lest the Christian character of our Church should have deteriorated, and, as a consequence, the Missionary spirit be on the decline amongst her members; or that God had withheld his blessing from us, and that our Missionary exertions were ceasing to exercise a beneficial influence on the state of the world, and were, therefore, deemed unworthy of that liberal and persevering support from the Wesleyan Community which the other Societies were receiving from the Churches to which they respectively belong. The very extent of the pressure, considered in connexion with the general state of this particular Society, proves that such is not the case. The difficulty is a general one, and so is the cause which has produced it.

What is this cause? What has produced this state of things? Why are the funds of the Wesleyan Missionary Society insufficient to meet the claims which are made upon them?

These pecuniary difficulties cannot with justice be ascribed to neglect or imprudence on the part of the Committees, to which, from time to time, the Conference has intrusted the management of the Missionary Department of our Connexional Affairs: for, although in the direction of matters of such great magnitude, and with which perplexing and difficult questions are frequently blended,—affecting, as they do, so many different classes of men, and involving the destinies of eternity, as well as the interests of time,—mistakes and errors are unavoidable; yet the present state of the Society's Missions bears the fullest testimony to the care and fidelity with which its affairs have, from the commencement of its operations, been constantly conducted. The published proceedings of the Society forbid the indulgence of evil surmisings and suspicions on this question. These show that the successive Committees, having undertaken, with singleness of eye, the responsible duties assigned to them by the Conference, have been "guided in judgment," and taught "in the way," by Him whose prerogative it is to give "the wisdom which is profitable to direct;" and that, in the fear of the Lord, they have vigilantly guarded the holy work intrusted to their charge, and have faithfully administered the means placed at their disposal, in promoting the great cause of human salvation.

Nor are the financial embarrassments, which are at present felt by the Society, attributable to a falling off in the amount of its Annual Receipts. It is only due to the Christian charity of the Wesleyan Body to record, that, in the midst of the severe distress with which this country, on several occasions, has been visited, the Missionary contributions of its members and friends have not been diminished. On more than one occasion, during the last quarter of a century, the agricultural interests of the nation have suffered from different causes; our commercial energy and industry have been enfeebled and paralyzed; poverty has pressed heavily upon the manufacturing classes in several parts of the kingdom; the most promising speculations have failed, and their failure has entailed destitution and suffering upon multitudes; but during no one of these periods has the Income of the Wesleyan Missionary Society declined.   Amidst these difficulties, the flow of liberality in this channel has steadily increased, and has conveyed the "living water" of the Gospel into countries where the people were perishing for lack of this great "gift of God."   Even during the past year of almost unexampled anxiety and distress, the Income of the Society has been increased; and in not a few instances, "the very depths of the poverty" of the people have "abounded to the riches of their liberality," in making provision for the relief of the "world" which "lieth in wickedness."   These facts furnish a noble proof of the firm hold which the Missionary cause has taken on the judgment and conscience of that portion of the flock of Christ to which we belong, as well as a satisfactory earnest that the members of our Body, assisted as they have been by generous friends belonging to other denominations, will do still greater things than we have yet witnessed for the extension of the kingdom of the Redeemer.   It is well that, by the blessing of God, so much has been attempted and accomplished by the instrumentality of Wesleyan Methodism; but we believe, that there is a heart in those who are connected with it to do more, and that the ability will not be found wanting.   While they continue to give utterance, in the great congregation, and around the domestic altar, to the truly Missionary sentiments and feelings which are embodied in our sacred hymns and "spiritual songs," they will not fail to do that which in them lieth to fill the heavenly fold of the good Shepherd. Undoubtedly, they will not cease to be practically consistent; and while they sing,—

> " Our gracious Master, and our God,
>   Assist us to proclaim,
> To spread through all the earth abroad,
>   The honours of thy name ; "

they will be found doing their utmost to make the " way " of the Lord " known upon earth," and " his saving health among all nations," that " the people may praise Him ; yea, that all the people may praise Him."

The embarrassments of the Society have not been produced by an extravagant expenditure of moneys, either at home or abroad. On this, as well as on all other points, the proceedings of the Committee will endure the most searching investigation, and the most rigid scrutiny, on the part of friends or of foes. It is, indeed, generally admitted, that the expenditure of the Wesleyan Missionary Society is conducted with the strictest regard to economy ; and that such is the case, is demonstrated by the fact, that, notwithstanding the care with which other Missionary Institutions disburse their respective incomes, there is not one which supports so many establishments, and such a number of Missionaries and other Agents, abroad, at so small an amount of expense to the Parent Society.

There is no unnecessary expenditure of money for home purposes. The valuable services of the Treasurers are bestowed gratuitously. The Secretaries only receive the same moderate allowances which are usually granted to Wesleyan Ministers having similar domestic claims, which allowances constitute the entire amount of their official income. The salaries of the Clerks employed at the Mission-House are fixed at the lowest possible amount, considering the nature and extent of the duties which they have to perform ; and those Ministers who plead the cause of the Society, and to whom it is placed under such deep obligations, receive nothing more from the Auxiliary Institutions which they visit, than the sum necessary to defray the expenses which they incur in travelling from place to place ; while on many of the Circuits and Stations, the Anniversaries of the minor Associations connected with them are held at little or no expense. If, under any circumstances, more money is spent in any particular locality than is really necessary, it is when our friends, from a laudable desire to render the Anniversary services as interesting and beneficial as possible, invite a greater number of Ministers than is really necessary. There is reason to believe, that this does sometimes happen; and when it does, it operates unfavourably in more than one respect. In addition to the expense of which it is the cause, the pressure of many speakers prevents any one of them from entering so much at length into the topics suitable to the occasion, as it is proper that some one of the number should do, in order that, as far as is possible, justice may be done to the character of the cause itself, and that strong and definite impressions may be made on the minds of the hearers, in reference to the grandeur and blessedness of its results, as well as to the claims of Christian duty and obligation, in connexion with the recovery of the world to the dominion of Him on whose " head " are " many crowns." Each speaker is grieved, because he feels that *his* presence, at least, was not necessary; and the people are disappointed in their expectat'ons. On such occasions, it may, perhaps, happen, that a witty anecdote may excite a smile or a laugh; a pretty figure of speech, or a pithy saying, may gain the admiration of a few; but the cause is not effectually served; the business of the Society does not go on as it should do; no encouraging results are realized. The wrong end of the telescope is placed before the eye of the congregation; and every thing connected with our Missionary Stations appears to be small and remote, instead of being displayed in the fulness of their proportions, and brought near to the minds and hearts of the beholders. With great deference to the opinions of others, it may be stated, as the result of much observation, that while it has seldom happened that a Meeting has suffered for want of adequate help, failures have frequently been occasioned by a superabundant supply. Let all be taught to give rather for the sake of the Master, than on account of the servant by whom He is, at best, but unworthily represented; and when we have learned to do every thing " as unto the Lord, and not as unto men," the expenses of all our religious Anniversaries will be materially lessened.

All the means that prudence and experience can supply are employed to guard against an improvident expenditure of money abroad. A certain portion of the income of the Society is appropriated to each foreign District, by the General Committee; which grant is made with a due regard to the funds of the Society, and to the relative claims of each District. In every foreign District-Meeting it is a part of the ordinary business to make a prospective distribution of this grant from the Committee amongst the Circuits belonging to each District. In order that this distribution may be made as equitably and satisfactorily as possible, it is preceded by an inquiry into the circumstances of all the Stations, and also into the probable amount of allowances to which each Missionary will be entitled during the year for which the arrangement is made. At the following District-Meeting, an account, from each Circuit or Station, of the RECEIPTS and DISBURSEMENTS OF EVERY KIND, duly prepared, is presented, and is carefully investigated by the Chairman, in the presence of the Meeting. If, after such examination, the entries are found to be in exact accordance with the authorized scale of allowances, it is passed, and officially signed by the Chairman and Secretary of the Meeting; but if not, it is referred for amendment, and is afterwards duly authenticated by the signatures of the proper authorities. Thus prepared, the accounts are forwarded to the Secretaries in London, with the other District-Minutes, and the Reports of the state of the societies and schools. After an analysis of each account has been prepared, the whole of the details are reviewed, examined, and, when necessary, compared with those of the previous year, by the Sub-Committee of Finance, appointed for that purpose; by whom a Report is made to the General Committee, in which is embodied a statement of such errors as may have been found in any of the Accounts, and of the charges, if any, which are judged to be unauthorized, unnecessary, or excessive, with such general remarks and observations as may be deemed necessary. After this Report has been received and adopted by the General Committee, it is, with all convenient speed, transmitted to the Chairman of the District to which it relates, accompanied by a suitable letter from the Secretaries, in

which they dilate more largely on the various topics which
are contained in the Report itself, for the purpose of having these documents laid before the following District-
Meeting, for inquiry and explanation. If the official
replies to them are not satisfactory to the Committee, the
claim or claims are disallowed; and should the amount
have been received, it is charged to the personal account
of the proper party, by whom, in due time, the sum is
repaid to the Treasurers. Of course, such an arrangement
as this greatly adds to the duties of the Secretaries and
others at the Mission-House; but then it will at once
be seen, that it must be attended with immense advantages, in a financial point of view, to the interests of the
Society. Such a regular and precise examination as
that which this mode of proceeding renders necessary,
secures, on the part of Missionaries, and the other Agents
of the Society abroad, the observance of great accuracy
and economy in all their pecuniary transactions with the
Committee in this country. Nor should it be forgotten,
that it brings the monetary claims, made on account of
each Station, under the review of two parties who are the
most likely to examine them carefully, and to detect any
error or mistake in them; that is to say, the General
Committee in England, and the Foreign District-Meet-
ings. It will be readily conceived, that, apart from higher
considerations, the constant pressure felt by the Parent
Committee, in consequence of the inadequacy of the
income of the Society to meet the regular and undoubted
claims that are made upon its funds, urges them to exercise the utmost vigilance in keeping the Missionary
exchequer, of which they are the appointed and responsible guardians; and as it is almost an invariable result,
that the pecuniary grants which are made to the respective Districts leave deficiencies unprovided for, if it should
happen that a Missionary belonging to any one of them has
become extravagant in some part of his expenditure, the
Circuit-account will discover that to his brethren; who,
having themselves deficiencies which the grant is too
small to cover, will not fail to disallow every improper or
excessive charge. If, therefore, no loftier motive governed

the proceedings of the Missionaries in this matter than a regard for their personal interest, even in that case the necessities of some would furnish an effectual pledge for an economical procedure on the part of all the members of any particular District-Meeting. Indeed, while the Society continues to maintain and support its present establishments at the same amount of outlay, or a less or greater number at a proportionate rate, any considerable waste or excess in the disbursement of the funds will be impracticable. In such a magnificent undertaking as this in which we have embarked, contingencies are constantly occurring, which no human foresight can anticipate, or skill, on the part of those who conduct it, prevent or avoid. The places of deceased and enfeebled Missionaries must be supplied, and the expenses occasioned by sickness and other causes must be paid. The claims of the widows and orphans of those faithful men who have sickened and died in foreign climes, cannot be overlooked. In remote and uncivilized regions, buildings of various kinds must be erected and repaired. Large sums are, of necessity, expended on the preparation, outfit, and passage of Missionaries proceeding to foreign lands, as well as in connexion with their return to their native country. Other expenses are incurred at home, for the purpose of keeping the moral machine in a state of vigorous and effective operation, especially those which are connected with the press. The processes of nature teach us, that, if we would reap, we should sow; that, if we would gather, we should scatter abroad: for "there is that scattereth, and yet increaseth; and there is that withholdeth more than is meet, and it tendeth to poverty unto him." In addition to all these sources of expenditure, seven printing establishments had to be maintained abroad; three hundred Day- and Sunday-schools had to be fostered; three hundred and sixty-seven Missionaries, with their families, had to be provided for, and three hundred and thirty-six salaried teachers supported; at a time when the entire income of the Society amounted to little more than ninety thousand pounds.

VI.

THE foregoing observations have not been made because it is felt that any defence of the proceedings of the Society at home, or of its agents abroad, is needed ; but for the purpose of communicating information, which, it is hoped, will not be regarded as either unseasonable or unwelcome. The age in which it is our providential lot to live and act, is distinguished by a spirit of earnest and persevering inquiry ; and, as this spirit is found in the church, as well as in general society, it is much to be desired that every thing connected with the great religious movement which is now taking place for the conversion of all nations to the faith of the Redeemer, should be well known and understood, especially by his faithful and devoted servants, in order that they may " know how " they " ought to answer every man."

Still, the question returns, What has produced these embarrassments ? The reply to it is, that the pecuniary difficulties of which the Wesleyan Missionary Society now complains are felt, at least, in the same degree, by the other Missionary institutions; and may be traced to a COMMON CAUSE, which is, *the success with which, by the effectual blessing of God, they have been honoured and rewarded.* In the affairs of this life, when men succeed in their mercantile engagements and pursuits, just in proportion as they prosper they are relieved from those difficulties to which they are not unfrequently exposed at the outset of their career, and secure for themselves, as the reward of their integrity and industry, a quiet and dignified retirement. Far different is the case with respect to the Missionary enterprise. In this undertaking, SIGNAL SUCCESS IS THE PRECURSOR OF SIGNAL EMBARRASSMENT. This may appear to be a paradox ; but it is one of those evangelical paradoxes which are often met with, and may be as clearly and satisfactorily demonstrated as that by which we are taught, that when the believer is " weak," then is he " strong." Startling, therefore, and perhaps incredible, as this view of the case may be, even to persons who have not been altogether inattentive to these subjects, it will occasion no surprise to those who have carefully studied the genius of Christianity, as it has been developed in the mode and results of its working in ancient and in modern times.

When the Gospel is introduced into a country, and operates effectually, by the power of the Holy Ghost, one of the very earliest salutary effects that it produces, is, a desire for the knowledge and enjoyment of the blessings which it unfolds, and which it is designed to bestow upon our race. In proportion as the spiritual privileges of " the common salvation" are understood and appreciated, by the people to whom they are offered, this desire is diffused and strengthened. Conformably with the high commission received by St. Paul " from the Lord," that great Apostle devoted himself to the work of making " known to the Gentiles the unsearchable riches of Christ." He succeeded in his Mission. At Philippi, at Thessalonica, at Berea, at Antioch, at Ephesus, and even at Athens, with her science, her literature, her unrivalled specimens of art, and her thirty thousand altars, erected to as many distinct divinities, the hearts of not a few of the inhabitants were drawn out in earnestness of desire after " the doctrine of salvation" which Paul preached. Christian communities were formed, under his care and direction, in these and in other places, until, in his case, as in that of the Missionary Societies of the present day, one of the fruits of the triumphs which he had been enabled to gain " in every place" was, an increase of labour and anxiety; for, when enumerating his various cares and toils, he mentions, as one of the greatest of them all, " that which cometh upon me daily,—the care of all the churches."

Let us turn our attention to modern Missionary efforts. At the period of their commencement, the heathen world was in an apathetic state. The generation that then existed in the midst of different forms of pagan idolatry, all inseparable from many inexpressible evils and crimes, were not less the victims of ignorance and depravity, acted upon by a Satanic agency, than are the men now living in those countries. Nay, they were much more ignorant and depraved. The present generation are, in many instances, deriving advantages from the indirect influence of Christianity, which were unknown to their ancestors. But while the former were satisfied, or, at least, seemed to have been indifferent, or, in other words, did not know that they had a Father in heaven who had mercifully provided " better things " for them, and, therefore, did not desire or seek for them,—cries for relief are now heard issuing from regions where unbroken silence formerly prevailed. The dumb wastes of misery have found a voice; and not from one place, but from many, that voice is heard, saying to the churches of Britain, " Come over and help us." This touching request is the result of the faith and labours of Missionaries. It is at once a proof of their fidelity and usefulness, and the prelude and pledge of ultimate and complete success.

VII.

THE fruits of Christian instruction, especially amongst a people just emerging, by the instrumentality of the Gospel, from a state of barbarism, naturally attract the attention of neighbouring tribes, and lead them to inquire into the cause by which such wonderful things have been accomplished. Although it should always be remembered, that the primary object for which Missionaries are sent forth is, to " turn men from darkness to light, and from the power of Satan unto God, that they may receive forgiveness of sins, and inheritance among them who are sanctified by faith that is in " Christ Jesus; it should also be borne in mind, as a well-ascertained and well-established fact, that, in the same measure in which they succeed in securing the principal object that they have in view, other results are realized, which, though of a subordinate character, because connected with this life only, exercise a most beneficial influence upon the personal and social condition of the people to whom they make known that great mystery of God, " which had been hid from ages and from generations." Christianity is the parent of real civilization. It is in the order of God that it should be so. He who made the world in conformity with his own infinitely wise conceptions, has saved, is yet saving, and will save mankind, by his own gracious plans and institutions, from the evils which sin and transgression have produced, that in all things He may be glorified. As God the Creator, he produces manifold results by one simple principle, as, for instance, by that of vegetation; and as God the Redeemer, he makes it manifest, that "the foolishness of God is wiser than men, and the weakness of God stronger than men," by communicating to man, however low he may have fallen, through the manifestation of "the truth as it is in Jesus," every thing that is necessary to his real security, dignity, and happiness. When the "incorruptible seed" is sown in the heart, and "liveth and abideth" there, love to God, which is the element of holiness, springs up, and buds, and blossoms, with "whatsoever things are true, whatsoever things are honest, whatsoever things are just, whatsoever things are pure, whatsoever things are lovely, whatsoever things are of good report." In the same degree in which the individual members of a community are brought under the influence of this principle, its collective state will be improved, and the mass will partake of the character of the parts of which it is composed. Thus as "the word of the Lord" has "free course," and moves onward, every good thing follows in its train, attesting and gracing its progress; and when the saving knowledge which it reveals shall cover the earth, as the waters cover the great deep, the "people shall be all righteous," and the world, sanctified by the truth, will reflect the order and tranquillity, the purity and charity, of heaven. Then "judgment shall dwell in the wilderness, and righteousness remain in the fruitful field; and the work of righteousness shall be peace, and the effect of righteousness, quietness and assurance for ever."

It is not intended, by these observations, to discourage the use of all suitable means and appliances for the improvement of society, in subordination to the Gospel; but they are adduced for the purpose of showing, that, professedly and practically, they should always be regarded and employed as inferior and subordinate to "the law of the Lord," which "is perfect, converting the soul." Innumerable proofs of the beneficial influence of the Gospel are recorded in the journals of travellers, as well as in the archives of Missionary Societies, which can neither be successfully denied, nor ingeniously explained away. These have obtained for Christianity the laudations of men who entertain but little respect for it in its highest character,—as a revelation from God; but who, professing a desire to encourage social improvement of every kind, are willing to honour it, as one amongst other instrumentalities which they think may be employed, with equal success, in furtherance of their favourite object. We dare not do such dishonour to "the glorious Gospel of the ever-blessed God," as to accept the tender of such homage as that on its behalf. It is not merely a moral power, but THE power, "the power of GOD," and "the power of God unto salvation to every one that believeth," whatever may have been his former state and condition. It is just as impossible for man to provide an effectual substitute for the Gospel, as it would be for him to produce an effectual substitute for the sun which God has created and made for the "rule of the day." Jehovah will not give the "glory" of his creative acts, or, what is still greater, of his redeeming purposes and operations, "to another;" and as "the heavens" now "declare the glory of the Lord, and the firmament showeth his handywork," so when "the end" shall come, the divinely-appointed agency will be so manifestly seen in the accomplishment of the divinely-promised result,—the creation of "new heavens, and a new earth, wherein" shall dwell "righteousness,"—that "every creature" shall be heard, saying, "Blessing, and honour, and glory, and power, be unto Him that sitteth upon the throne, and unto the Lamb for ever and ever."

Such is the great purpose of God; and it cannot be set aside by secular educational schemes, by stringent laws and regulations, by political changes, or by any human plans and expedients, however specious or popular. To think that it may be rendered void, is to "imagine a vain thing," at which "He who sitteth in the heavens shall laugh." If the raging waves of the sea can pass over "the sand" which the Most High hath "appointed to be the boundary thereof," then may man, by methods of his own devising, set aside the decree of God,—that "men shall be blessed," yea, and blessed only in and by the Gospel of his Son. That is the true source of all improvement; the great moral Nile, that enriches every country through which it flows, and clothes it with fertility and beauty. Wherever "the streams" of the "river" which "maketh glad the city of God" have not yet found their way, all things wear the aspect of a desolate wilderness.

VIII.

HERE we appeal to living witnesses. A Missionary is established in an uncivilized region of the globe, and some of its inhabitants are converted. "The law of the Spirit of life in Christ Jesus" makes them "free from the law of sin and death." Thus the great design is, to some extent, secured; and, as the consequence of that, the man who, before he became the subject of this spiritual change, wrapped himself in his kaross, or wandered about almost (if not altogether) naked, is clothed. He who before lodged with the wild beast in his lair, now reposes in his own cottage, which shelters his family, as well as himself. Instead of roaming in the wilderness, in search of the means of support, or preying upon his neighbour, he tends his flocks, or cultivates his fields and garden, that he may "provide things honest in the sight of all men." The man never felt his need of a home, until he became a Christian. Then he desired a place of residence; and he did so, in order that he might be taught "the way of God more perfectly," and have a school, in which his children should be instructed. Religious considerations lead to a change of practice, and, finally, to a change of habit, in matters connected with the present state; and bind the individual to a new course of conduct, productive of a large amount of domestic happiness and enjoyment. "I understand," said Shawundais, (John Sunday,) the converted Indian Chief, to a congregation which he was called to address at Plymouth, in the year 1837:—"I understand, that many of you are disappointed, because I have not brought my Indian dress with me. Perhaps, if I had it on, you would be afraid of me. Do you wish to know how I dressed when I was a pagan Indian? I will tell you. My face was covered with red paint. I stuck feathers in my hair. I wore a blanket and leggings. I had silver ornaments on my breast; a rifle on my shoulder; a tomahawk and scalping-knife in my belt. That was my dress then. Now, do you wish to know why I wear it no longer? You will find the cause in Second Corinthians, fifth chapter, and seventeenth verse : ' Therefore, if any man be in Christ, he is a new creature: old things are passed away: behold, all things are become new.' When I became a Christian, feathers and paint done away. I gave my silver ornaments to the Mission cause. Scalping-knife done away; tomahawk done away: that my tomahawk now," said he, holding up, at the same time, a copy of the Ten Commandments, in the Ojibewa language. " Blanket done away. Behold," he exclaimed, in a manner in which simplicity and dignity of character were combined,—" behold, all things are become new." New, indeed; and not in his case only, but in that of multitudes of reclaimed savages—under the care of Protestant Missionary Societies—throughout the world. Thus, on Mission Stations, the germ of all real improvement is found in connexion with the Gospel of Christ ;—schools, presses, agricultural operations, pastoral pursuits, and even mercantile transactions. These new lights are seen from afar, by tribes who are still in that state of ignorance and wretchedness from which their brethren have been graciously rescued by the arm of the Lord ; or intelligence is conveyed to them of the wonderful works which have been wrought. Their curiosity is awakened ; and, like the eastern Magi, who were led by the unknown star to Bethlehem, to behold the new-born Saviour of men, the Heathens repair to the scene of Missionary triumph, that they may see with their own eyes the things of which they had before heard, and, " falling down on their faces, worship"—to them " the unknown"—" God, and acknowledge, that God is there of a truth." They are ignorant, indeed, of the spiritual principles at work in the hearts of those around them ; they have no just conceptions of the agency by which the " new creation" they behold has

been effected ; but they can and do appreciate the sub-
stantial proofs of its reality, which they perceive in the
improved condition of their fellow-men, who were once
as miserable as themselves. On inquiring into the cause
of this change, and learning that the Gospel has produced
it, they entreat that a Missionary may be sent to instruct
them, that they also may be blessed. Nothing will satisfy
them but a promise, that their request shall be conveyed
over " the great waters," to the good people of England. In
this way, the marked success of the great enterprise is constantly multiplying demands for labourers to enter into
other fields which are " white unto the harvest." The
world, awakened to a sense of its wants, is knocking at the
gates of our churches, and is perpetually inquiring, " Who
will show us any good ? " Earnest cries for help are waft-
ed to our shores by almost every breeze. One of our
Missionaries, that he might induce a New-Zealand Chief
to await with patience the arrival of a Teacher, reminded
him, that " when the tide ebbs, it flows again." " I know
it," replied the Chief; " but when will the tide flow that
is to bring us a Missionary?" "I am the Chief of a
numerous people," said an aged Indian warrior to a Missionary on the Manatulan islands, in the summer of
1840; " and I wish them to be instructed. We have
heard, that our brothers who are near the White Settle-
ments have received the Great Word. We have heard
that the Great Spirit has told the white man to send that
Word to all his red children : why does he not send it to
us ? I have been looking many moons down the river, to
see the Missionary's canoe; but it has not come yet."
This supernatural desire is spreading in both hemispheres :
and such a desire as this—one so earnest, so importunate,
so manifestly divine—cannot, must not, will not be
denied. It is communicated to Missionary Boards in the
letters of individual Missionaries; in documents of a more
general and official character ; in the form of petitions, as
well as in thrilling appeals, from the people themselves.
And the efforts which have been made to comply with it,
have mainly contributed to involve the Missionary Societies in their present pecuniary difficulties.

c

IX.

RECOGNISING in this desire for Christian Missionaries, which has originated in the success of Missions, the voice of God responding to the prayers of his people, and approving of their exertions to make his name known amongst the Gentiles, the Committee of the Wesleyan Missionary Society resolved to make a great effort to meet a fervent wish, which they had contributed to produce and cherish. This intention on the part of the Committee was publicly and formally announced; and the obligations which such a step, taken in advance by the Society, would impose upon the contributors to its funds, to increase the amount of their subscriptions and donations, were distinctly stated at the Anniversaries of the Society and of its principal Auxiliaries throughout the kingdom, as well as in the Official Publications of the Parent Institution.

The Report for the year ending April, 1836, contains the following ingenuous and explicit declaration :—

"The Committee owe it to themselves, and to the work with which they are officially connected, to make it known to all their friends, that, whilst the recent history of these important Missions has furnished much occasion for holy joy and gratitude, it has brought with it, to *them* at least, occasions of serious and embarrassing anxiety, arising out of those very circumstances which are so generally and properly adduced as themes of gratulation and of praise. Never, indeed, did they more deeply feel the difficulty of the post which they have occupied; as being, on the one hand, responsible to the Society for every new and additional expenditure of money; whilst, on the other hand, they have been still more solemnly responsible to God for an obedient and grateful use of those important openings for extended usefulness which have been set before them. In this dilemma, they have often felt great delicacy, in proceeding to involve the Society beforehand in any plans which were likely to entail a considerable addition to the annual charges on its funds; and yet they could not close their eyes against the danger which existed, of their sinning against the providence of God, as well as against the zeal and charity which have hitherto supplied resources for the maintenance of every enterprise in which the Committee have, year after year, ventured to engage. It is, therefore, a great relief to them, that, ere they commit themselves more fully and decisively to any permanent augmentation of the Society's labours and expenditure, they have the opportunity of appealing, in this public and formal manner, to the Society at large, and to their representatives, now assembled from various parts of the empire, as to the course which, under existing circumstances, it is their duty to pursue. That many, yea, most of the foreign

Stations already established require a speedy re-inforcement, and that a considerable number of places not yet occupied are presenting calls on the Society, which must not—or cannot, at least, without guilt in some quarter—be neglected any longer, are facts which cannot be denied."

The intentions of the Committee, as thus announced, were universally approved by the friends of the Society. It was felt by them all, that " the set time " had come for re-inforcing and extending our Missions, more especially in the once slave-colonies of the Crown, and in those parts of the Mission field towards which the agents of " the Man of Sin" were beginning to direct their attention and efforts, with that zeal and subtlety for which they have always been distinguished.

Thus encouraged, the Committee at once proceeded to extend the sphere of the Society's operations. In addition to thirty-seven Missionaries (twenty-two of whom were married) sent out in the course of the year 1835-36, thirty-nine persons, including Missionaries and their wives, embarked for various Stations during the following year. To these, forty-eight were added within the succeeding twelve months. To supply losses occasioned by sickness, death, and other causes, as well as to meet new and urgent applications for help, a large supply of Missionaries was sent out in 1838-39; and a still larger one in the course of the year 1839-40,' during which period twenty-nine married and nineteen single Missionaries were sent into the foreign work. From this statement it appears, that, including Missionaries and the wives of Missionaries, within the brief period of six years, two hundred and eighty-nine individuals were sent to Stations in all the five great divisions of the globe, to promote the purposes contemplated by the Wesleyan Missionary Society. Generous and noble efforts! In the circumstances under which they were made, they well became a people, the object of whose religious union, from the commencement of their history until the present time, has been *the spread of scriptural holiness at home and abroad, by the dissemination of evangelical truth,* and who avow, that " the world is their parish." The pecuniary bearing of these great exertions was speedily felt by the funds of the Society, and was exhibited, from year to year, in the published Balance-Sheet. The balance, in the hands of the Treasurers, on the General Account, which, at the beginning of the year 1835, amounted to nearly nine thousand pounds, was, at the close of the year 1836, reduced to little more than six thousand. When the end of the following year arrived, it was found, that there was a balance AGAINST the Treasurers, on the General Account, amounting to forty-five pounds, twelve shillings, and eight pence. During the ensuing twelve months, that Deficiency was increased to between nine and ten thousand pounds : in 1839, it amounted to more than twice that sum ; and at the end of the year 1840, the real debt, due by the Society, exceeded thirty thousand pounds. Nor will this growing expenditure excite surprise, when it is considered, that, in addition to the Society's having to provide, in whole or in part, the means of support for such an increased number of Missionaries and their families, a large expense was, of necessity, incurred, in sending them to their respective places of destination. Moderate as is the outfit of wearing apparel and books granted to Missionaries, and great as is the care that is taken to procure passages for them at the lowest rate consistent with their comfort and security, the charges for passage and outfit, from the beginning of the year 1836 to the close of 1840, amounted to twenty-six thousand, six hundred and seventy-nine pounds, six shillings. The expense incurred by sending out such a large number of married and single Missionaries, during the period to which reference has just been made, and the permanent additional annual outlay, rendered necessary by such an extension of the work, unavoidably involved the Society in debt, and increased its annual disbursements to an extent much beyond the amount of its annual receipts, as had been foreseen by the Missionary Committee, and announced by them in their Report, already quoted.

The Missionaries who have gone out during the last seven years, have not been sent to Stations where they were neither needed nor desired: they went forth in compliance with loud, earnest, and repeated entreaties; and the localities to which they were appointed are, in point of fact, the very places whence the most urgent calls are now addressed to the Committee for additional help, and where the operations of the Society are most seriously impeded, in consequence of the paucity of Ministers of the word of life. In Jamaica, to say nothing of the other West-India Districts, fifteen additional Missionaries are immediately required. At the Gambia, and Sierra-Leone, excessive labour, combined with the deadly influence of the climate, is exhausting the far too few devoted men who are connected with those Missions. The thousands who have been brought into the Redeemer's fold in the Friendly Islands, stand in need of more pastoral instruction and oversight; the Missionary force belonging to this Society in the East Indies is wholly inadequate to the efficient occupancy of the various posts amongst which it is distributed; and, indeed, from every District in every part of the world, if not from every Station, the Missionaries complain of their utter inability, in consequence of the comparative smallness of their number, to meet the claims that are perpetually made upon their time and services. Of this the following extracts from the communications of some of those excellent men will afford sufficient evidence.

" I do hope British Christians will turn their attention in a special manner to France and Switzerland, where so great and effectual a door is now opened. May all who have the means of increasing their subscriptions, be enlightened as to the extent of their duty, that the regular income of the Society may be sufficiently augmented, to allow you to assist in meeting the spiritual wants of the Continent! "—*Extract of a Letter from Lausanne, dated March 11th*, 1841.

" It is the opinion of this Meeting, that the work of God will be greatly promoted by the appointment of a second Missionary to the Mahaica Station; and that, unless such appointment take place, the people will greatly suffer, not only from the want of pastoral attention, but from the circulation of sentiments which we believe to be both erroneous and dangerous, and by which some of our members have been induced to leave us."—*Extract from the Demerara District-Minutes for* 1840.

" Even before our late deprivations, we had not nearly a sufficient number of Missionaries to carry on the affairs of the Mission with becoming vigour. Mr. Greenwood died in January. I have succeeded in obtaining a temporary supply for Black-River; but in the event of either his death or removal, I know not what to do, or where to look for a supply for Mr. Lewis. That the Committee are in difficulties, I know; and that it would afford them more pleasure to send, than to withhold, a proper number of Missionaries, I firmly believe; but really, while enlargement is viewed as out of our power, are we not to have the places of men filled up who are called to their endless rest? Is the Mission to go to absolute and irretrievable ruin?"—*Extract of a Letter from the Chairman of the Jamaica District, dated August 7th, 1841.*

"In Jaffna we need another English Missionary. If you could visit our Jaffna Mission-premises, I am sure you would decide at once on sending us help. We must maintain our Tamul work in energetic operation. Our School system must not decline, but rather be increased in its efficiency. We must have in connexion with it an English service, and a pastoral oversight: and we must occupy a leading place among the Missions, in the general plans of operation for the diffusion of the Gospel, in North Ceylon and South India."—*Extract of a Letter from Jaffna, dated June 28th, 1841.*

"I was sorry to see, from your last instructions, that your funds were in such a state, that you were obliged to require us to keep within our present expenditure. I cannot carry on the work which is now opening before me without additional help, and, of course, without additional expense. It will require a journey of more than one hundred miles, through dense jungle, to visit all the people that have lately been brought to Christianity; and if the work should extend to the south, as I expect it will, a journey of two hundred miles will not carry us round. And these journeys must be taken, or the people will be left as sheep without a shepherd. I can get a great deal of assistance near home, without any expense; but not for the jungle. I hope, under these circumstances, you will augment your pecuniary aid. I think, for the present, we can raise helpers on the spot.

"Perhaps you will say, 'Cannot they help themselves?' They cannot at present. They have little more property than the elephants, bears, and tigers, among which they live."—*Extract of a Letter from North Ceylon, dated April 8th, 1841.*

"The Committee have surely made up their minds to send us a reinforcement, and that right soon.

"I must remind the Committee, that Mr. Hodson is alone at Mysore, (as to European help,) and that Mr. Griffith is in the same situation at Negapatam; and that, considering the low state of health to which Mr. Griffith was reduced at the close of the last year, and the somewhat precarious state of Mr. Hodson's health, there will be considerable hazard in both cases, (unless a second man be sent as soon as possible to each of these two places,) not only to the brethren themselves, but also to the work which they are so hopefully conducting. The help to which I have referred is immediately required."—*Extract of a Letter from the General Superintendent of the Wesleyan East-Indian Missions, dated April 21st, 1841.*

" Quest. What towns, villages, or plantations, in the neighbourhood of each Station, are not yet visited ? give the reasons why they are not ; and state whether the said reasons are satisfactory to the brethren of the District ?

"Answer. The brethren do what they can ; and the reasons why many places are unvisited, and others but partially supplied, are perfectly satisfactory to the brethren of the District.   There are no obstacles of a providential nature in Southern Africa.   God has made the way plain, and opened access to every tribe ; and they cry, and their cry is loud and appalling, and in many instances it must daily be, alas ! a last despairing cry ; for, it seems, this cry for help to favoured Christendom must still be, to a considerable extent, in vain. ' But thou hast delivered thy soul.' "—*Extract from the Cape of Good Hope District-Minutes.*

" As Capai is so urgent in his requests for a Missionary, and has sent so repeatedly to me to know when he is to expect one, I have promised him to forward his request to the Committee.

" This large tribe of people are entirely without the means of religious instruction, and are in the grossest darkness, ' without hope, and without God in the world;' and hundreds are yearly carried into eternity, while they are as ignorant of eternal things as the beasts that perish.   They are the most warlike and savage of all the tribes of Kaffraria, and are more dreaded by their neighbours than any other people. Indeed, they are so intent on war and plunder, that they are seldom quiet for *four months* together without making their savage attacks on other tribes ; in which they are too often successful in plundering all they meet with, murdering the old people, and taking the young into captivity.   Accumulating large herds of cattle by these horrid means, their conquered and impoverished neighbours go and unite with them ; when generally they are well received by Capai, as he is always anxious to augment his power.

" Yet, under all these circumstances, the door is open for the Gospel of our Redeemer ; and the Chief is anxiously waiting to know, when and whether he can have a *Teacher to teach him and his people the great news from heaven.* A short time ago, he sent to me in a very formal manner, stating, ' *For a long time I have asked for a Teacher, but to no purpose. All the other Chiefs have Teachers ; but I have none. It is true, I know I am born a sinner, and have a wicked heart ; but still, only give me a Teacher, and I am sure I will take care of him.'* "— *Extract of a Letter from Kafferland, dated Nov.* 12th, 1838.

" Without further preface, I feel it my duty to implore you to send us, as soon as possible after this reaches you, a re-inforcement of, at least, *six more Missionaries ;* two or three of them may be single men ; but, with less than six additional Missionaries, it will be quite impossible for us to occupy the large and promising field which now invites our labours.

" In *Kaffraria,* betwixt the Fish-River and the Zimvubu, (nearly three hundred miles,) we have, at present, only *five* regular Missionaries, with a few Catechists.   Now, we ought to have, at least, *twelve* Missionaries; but, with less than *eight*, it is impossible to occupy with efficiency our present ground. Indeed, unless a better supply can be afforded than our present complement of labourers, I incline to the opinion, that we had better abandon two or three of our existing Stations, and concentrate our Missionary force, so as to bear with greater effect upon a more limited population. For what is one Missionary to a *scattered* population of thirty or forty thousand Heathen, who must be taught even the first principles of Christian truth? Yet this disproportionate supply of labourers actually exists in our more remote Kaffer Missions. On the border of the colony, owing to the labours of other Societies, the paucity of Missionaries is not so great; but, even on the nearer Missions, an increase of labourers is highly desirable.

" We cannot go on much longer on the present plan. It appears to me like a want of good Missionary economy, to occupy *extensive fields inadequately ;* and, unless you can reinforce our numbers, we must withdraw some of the Missions, and strengthen the others. But will our people, will the friends of the Society who really care for the salvation of the souls of the Heathen, consent to such a measure? Has our zeal as Missionaries, and the desire of the native tribes for our labours, so far outrun the liberality of the Christian public at home, that we must not only stop further advances into the interior of this great continent, but also abandon in hopeless despair, to the great enemy of souls, the advanced posts which we already occupy? I must leave you, and the friends of our Missions, to answer this query.

" I waited patiently during 1837, because I saw you were engaged in a noble effort in behalf of India ; and I refrained from urging, as I ought, the wants and claims of South Africa in 1838, because I saw you were using your utmost efforts to provide for the Feejee islanders, and other parts of the South Seas. But now, in 1839, the Wesleyan Centenary year, I entreat you to think of poor Africa, with her millions of Heathen. Our present Missionary establishment is but an outline of what it should be, and what I and my respected brethren who commenced the various Missions always hoped it would become. For the last nineteen years I have never ceased to pray and to labour, that we might see an extensive Wesleyan Mission extending from Port-Elizabeth (Algoa-Bay) to Port-Natal, a distance of about seven hundred miles ; and, being a fine belt of country along the coast of South-eastern Africa, it is now, and always will be, one of the most thickly populated regions of Southern Africa.

" You will remember, that a request has also long appeared on our District-Minutes for a Missionary to be appointed to the tribe of Ncapai, beyond the Zimvubu river, and in the direction of Port-Natal. Recently another urgent application has been made from the Chief, through the Government-Agent, to the Colonial Government, requesting that the Governor would urge us to send him a Missionary. The Honourable Colonel Hare, the acting Lieutenant-Governor, has forwarded this request to me, expressing his desire, that, if possible, we would make arrangements to meet the wishes of the Chief. Mr. Fynn, the Government-

Agent, having stated his full conviction, that the Mission would do much good, and probably tend to the peace of that part of the country; I could only promise to lay the case before you: What do you say to this often-repeated request of a ferocious heathen Chief, now backed and supported by the Colonial Government ? I do confidently hope, that you will resolve on sending a Missionary for this large and powerful tribe, to whose case and country you will find an extended reference in the Minutes of our last District-Meeting."—*Extract of a Letter from the General Superintendent of the Wesleyan Missions in South-Eastern Africa, dated Port-Elizabeth, Algoa-Bay, July 27th,* 1839.

Appeals equally urgent and pressing from other portions of the Missionary field might easily be supplied; but it is deemed unnecessary to insert them, as those which have been selected afford a fair specimen of the whole, and are surely quite sufficient to awaken the deepest sympathy on behalf of the perishing Heathen. Here is a reply from " the Lord the SPIRIT" to the prayer of the church on behalf of the world. Is the church prepared for it? Reader, are you? This is only the first part of the answer. The desire which has been created is just beginning to make itself heard and felt. Most assuredly it will increase in energy and diffusiveness, until it shall become irresistible and universal; and all those who love the Lord Jesus Christ in sincerity and in truth, should prepare themselves for the new state of things which is approaching, and which is now nigh at hand, yea, " even at the doors."

While the Teachers already sent amongst the Heathen continue to be useful, applications of this kind will be multiplied. As long as God shall give testimony to the word of his grace, preached by his servants abroad, these requests will be urged. There is no other way to prevent them, than by the churches at home ceasing to pray for the spread of the Redeemer's kingdom in the earth; and by the Missionaries ceasing to labour for that object. This, however, will not be done. The people of God have taken the Mission cause, as it should be taken,—with all its contingencies; and they will abide by their choice. If spiritual prosperity lead to pecuniary embarrassment, they will still do their utmost to secure the desired success, and to remove the financial difficulties which it

may occasion, whenever or under whatever form they may
occur.

X.

THAT the success of Missionary Societies is the true
cause of these difficulties, is fully confirmed by facts connected with their history. So discouraging was the aspect
of affairs for some time after the commencement of the
Wesleyan Mission in New-Zealand, that the entire aban-
donment of that great enterprise of mercy was, at one
period, seriously contemplated by the Committee. But
He who has promised that " at eventide it shall be light,"
having tried the faith of his servants to the uttermost,
graciously interposed to prevent the execution of a design
which would have led to such disastrous results. After
years of trial, privation, and painful disappointments, the
good seed began to spring up; difficulties were removed;
restraints were imposed on the lawless passions of many
of the people; religious societies were formed; schools
were organized; and since the first appearance of these
gracious indications of a successful issue, Christianity has
achieved some of its greatest modern triumphs amongst
the once-cannibal and deeply-degraded barbarians of an
island, on whose shores, before the introduction of the
Gospel, nothing had been witnessed by European naviga-
tors, but deeds of such horrible atrocity that they may
not be named. A desire for Christian instruction now
pervades the length and breadth of the land, and mani-
fests itself in various ways, even in places where it was
least to be expected, as is shown by the following interesting statement, received from one of the Missionaries :—

"Leaving Rotoaera, we travelled nearly five days without meeting a
single inhabitant, or the vestige of a dwelling. Our road lay partly
along the foot of the snow-clad mountain, but chiefly through an extensive and uneven forest, whose close umbrageous foliage rendered it
almost impenetrable, even to the solar rays. This forest led us to the
winding and rapid river of Wanganui, whence our road lay along the
sea-coast to Port-Nicholson. Although in the interior the population is
so thin, here the people are very numerous. Along the coast, from
Wanganui to Waikanae, inclusive, a distance of about sixty miles over a
beautifully level and sandy beach, intersected by several small rivers,
there are, at the very lowest computation, three thousand souls; and

among them the same prevailing desire for religious instruction and books. I found a number of neat chapels in which they statedly assemble for worship; several of the people could read well, and many had learned to write. Of course much rudeness and ignorance still exist among them; but, considering their circumstances, having never been favoured with the direct instructions of an European Missionary, I could not but think them to be in a very pleasing and promising condition; and was often led to say, 'Behold, the fields are already white unto harvest.' I was received by them as a messenger from God; and could I have gratified their wishes by sojourning a while at each village, my journey would have been protracted indeed. This pleasing change is but of recent date, and was effected through the instrumentality of means apparently the most inefficient."

The writer, in describing the scenes he witnessed in another place, says,—

"I had no idea of meeting with any appearance of Christianity here; but my surprise was only equalled by my delight, when, on emerging from the dark shades of the dreary forest, the sonorous responses of this isolated people fell upon my ears; they were worshipping the God of heaven and of earth! They received me gladly; and I had an opportunity of unfolding to them the great truths of the Gospel, and supplying them with a few books. These people, like many others, have been persuaded to 'turn from idols to serve the living and true God,' through the instrumentality of our converted natives. On the following day, several of them accompanied us through the wood; where we found two more villages, the inhabitants of which were inquiring after the God of their salvation."—*Extract of a Letter from one of the Missionaries in New-Zealand.*

If the case were otherwise; if the attempt made to introduce the Gospel amongst the New-Zealanders had failed, and if the Missionaries had entirely abandoned the country fourteen years ago, as it was then feared they would be compelled to do, the Committee, instead of having to maintain in that District eleven Stations, fourteen Missionaries, and sixteen salaried Teachers, as well as to support a printing establishment, and many schools, at an expense of between five and six thousand pounds, would be involved in no expense whatever, in connexion with New-Zealand. But then there is another side to this question, which must be noticed. If this Mission had utterly failed, then those who are now sainted spirits, and who, during the last few years, have passed from our Missionary church there, in full assurance of faith, to the church triumphant in heaven, would, in all probability, have died in a state of ignorance and sinfulness, " without God, and without hope ; " the hundreds of the Aborigines who are united in church-fellowship at Hokianga, and elsewhere, and who, in a greater or less degree, enjoy and exhibit the gracious fruits of that change which the Gospel has effected in their condition, would have continued to be " filled with all unrighteousness, without natural affection, implacable, unmerciful ; " and the children, who are at present placed under a course of Christian instruction in the Mission schools, would have been left to grow up under the influence of the sanguinary and degrading customs of their ancestors.

Seven years since, a Wesleyan Missionary was sent to the Gold-Coast, under the express stipulation, that, if, within two or three months after his arrival, the prospect of usefulness should not be such as would justify him in remaining there, the gentleman at whose request he was sent thither, and who gave him a free passage in his own vessel, should bring him back to this country, without any charge to the Society. Mr. Dunwell, a most suitable person for such an undertaking, volunteered his services, and was appointed to that Station. He remained in the country, preaching the Gospel, until he was removed by death to another and a better world. Ere that event took place, the good seed sown by him had taken root ; and it has brought forth fruit, which remains until this day. That devoted Missionary has been succeeded by " faithful men," several of whom have also died ; but the work has steadily advanced ; and the success of the Mission has not only led to an enlargement of the sphere of the Society's operations on the Coast, but has been the means of opening the way for its Missionaries into the powerful kingdom of Ashantee ; for the benefit of which a special effort has already been made by the members of the Wesleyan Missionary Society, assisted by the friends of Africa belonging to other religious denominations. In this as in the former instance, the growth of the cause has added to our pecuniary liabilities and embarrassments. The experience of other Missionary Societies bears testimony to the accuracy of the opinion which is expressed in these pages on this point; in proof of which, it is only necessary to insert the following quotation from the last published Report of the Church Missionary Society :—

"The large amount of the Expenditure is to be traced to the progressive enlargement of most of the Missions, through the blessing from above which has been vouchsafed to their operations. At no antecedent period have the Missions, speaking of them as a whole, presented so favourable a view of the spiritual influence which they have been instrumental in diffusing."

The pecuniary embarrassments of that most useful institution have so increased since the Report from which the above extract has been taken was drawn up, that it has been deemed necessary, on the part of the General Committee, to publish an Address on the subject, in a late number of the "Church Missionary Record." That important document contains the following amongst other statements :—

"The financial situation of the Society has for some time occasioned great solicitude to the Committee. The difficulties in which they find themselves involved do not arise from a falling-off of income, but from that large increase of expenditure in the Missions, consequent on their progressive enlargement, and the success with which it has pleased God to bless the labours of his servants. Another cause of serious embarrassment to the Committee has been, the inadequacy of the funds available to meet the inequalities between income and expenditure in the course of the year.

"Though the Committee are deeply impressed with the obligation which is imposed on the Managers of a Missionary Society, on moral as well as financial grounds, to limit the expenditure, from year to year, within the income of the year; yet they equally feel, that the present state of the Society's operations, as well as of its finances, call for the use of all suitable means to enlarge that income.

"The utter inadequacy of the Society's income to meet the demands from abroad for Missionaries, has compelled the Committee to reject many appeals for the formation of new Missions, under very encouraging circumstances; and other similar ones are now before them, to which they have no alternative but to return the same painful reply.

"The pecuniary difficulties of the Committee have likewise been materially increased by the very success with which it has pleased God of late years to crown the Society's operations; by which the Missions have been rapidly enlarged, and a consequent increase of expenditure occasioned, especially in New-Zealand, Tinnevelly, and North India. The news of multitudes inquiring the way of salvation led the Committee to incur expenses, of which the extent was not fully foreseen, in their anxiety to meet the demand."

While, therefore, regret is felt and expressed, on account of the financial difficulties which press with so much weight on those noble Societies which are endeavouring to spread throughout the world "the faith once delivered to the saints," the churches may well rejoice in that which has produced them. It is because success is emblazoned on one side of the Missionary banner which Protestantism has unfurled, that monetary embarrassments are inscribed on the other. "Most gladly, therefore," even in the midst of trials, should we "glory" in a state of things which proves, that the "power of Christ" is resting upon "the work of our hands."

XI.

LARGE as is the debt which has been contracted by the Wesleyan Missionary Society, and desirable though it is that it should be liquidated with the least possible delay, it is a matter of much less anxiety than is the deficiency of its income, as compared with what it ought to be, in order that it may fully meet the increased and increasing demands which are made upon it. *The heart of Christianity has led the Society into debt ; and the heart of Christianity will provide for its complete extinction, in due time.* Leeds, in which the foreign Missions of the Connexion may be said to have originated, has already spoken out, in a manner worthy of itself, on this part of the case : the example which has been set in the West Riding of Yorkshire will unquestionably be imitated by the friends of Wesleyan Missions throughout the United Kingdom ; and the work will be done, and done promptly and effectually too.

That which imperatively demands earnest and practical attention is, the excess of the Missionary expenditure over the aggregate amount of receipts. This deficiency neither can nor ought to be allowed to continue any longer. No addition must be made to the existing debt. When the work of enlargement commenced, a few years ago, the reply to the statements which were then put forth by the Committee, in various quarters, was, "Show us that a great necessity exists, and we will make a suitable effort to meet it." The exigency of the case has been fully demonstrated; and now that the Centenary movement has terminated,—which, to some extent, at least, has, no doubt, affected the amount of contributions for Missionary purposes,*—renewed and more vigorous exertions should be made to maintain the position occupied by the Society, in the great Missionary army, which is asserting the honours, and spreading the victories, of the cross, amongst many different "nations, and kindreds, and people, and tongues;" unless, indeed, the Wesleyan Methodists are prepared to take a less prominent station, and to confess their inability to render more effective service to the common cause of the Redeemer.

Such an ignoble proceeding as the latter alternative involves, would be equally inconsistent with character and duty on the part of the Connexion. We owe much to our Lord; and we have many resources which may be devoted to his service. Having been employed as instruments for awakening others from their slumbers, and of rousing them to a state of activity in this holy warfare, deep and well-merited would our disgrace be, if, after all our professions, and all our exertions, we were to exhibit symptoms of indifference, or of indolence, in the presence of the "cloud of witnesses" with which we are encompassed, and at such a critical period in the great conflict which "the Lamb" is waging against his and our confederated foes. While the visitations of heaven, and the movements which are taking place on the earth, are summoning us to new enterprises of Christian zeal and benevolence, let us not act like Reuben, and Gilead, and Dan,

* Though the Centenary effort may, in some instances, have affected the amount of contributions to the Wesleyan Missionary Society, the Missions have derived great advantages from that noble movement. In addition to the commodious and central premises which have been gratuitously presented to the Society for the transaction of its business, munificent aid has been generously furnished by the Centenary Committee for the promotion of various objects exclusively Missionary in their character; not the least valuable of which is, the sum which has been granted for the purpose of assisting to provide a fund for the relief of the widows and orphans of deceased Missionaries.

and Asher, who, when called by Deborah and Barak to assist in the overthrow of the oppressors of Israel, disregarded the summons ; but let us imitate Ephraim, in which there " was a root against Amalek," and like Benjamin, and Machir, and Zebulun, and Naphtali, hasten " to the help of the Lord, to the help of the Lord against the mighty."

XII.

It may, perhaps, be asked by some of the persons to whom these observations are specially addressed, " Does the present state of the Society's Missions, as compared with their former condition, furnish such satisfactory evidence of growth and increase, as to justify the indulgence of a reasonable expectation, on our part, of securing, by the application of additional means, a wider diffusion of Christian knowledge, piety, and civilization ? Does a review of the success which has attended past efforts in this cause furnish good and sufficient reasons for continuing and increasing our exertions on its behalf ?" In replying to these, as well as to all similar, inquiries, it should be premised, that, if little or no visible good had been realized by our prayers and exertions, our duty and obligations to carry out the purposes of the Redeemer, by sending the Gospel into all the world, would be equally clear and binding. Success in this " work of faith " is cheering and animating : however, it should be distinctly understood, that it is not because we can show, in connexion with the work, manifest tokens of prosperity, that we are to prosecute it with untiring zeal and diligence ; but, because this is a duty which is enjoined upon us by the great Head of the church himself. " Go ye into all the world, and preach the Gospel to every creature," is a command binding upon individuals, and collective bodies of Christians, which cannot be neglected with impunity. To dissociate the obligation of duty to propagate the Gospel from the privilege connected with the possession of so invaluable a treasure, is impossible. The Sovereign Lawgiver has joined these two together ; and the church cannot put them asunder.

Here we may perceive and admire the harmony which

subsists between the counsels and the operations of the
Godhead. As we are taught by the Holy Spirit, that we
are " debtors both to the Greeks and to the Barbarians,
both to the wise .and to the unwise ;" so one of the
earliest and strongest desires which He produces in the
truly regenerate, is connected with the salvation of our
neighbour, and urges us to seek his good, by bringing him
under the influence of the Gospel of Christ. This feeling
is a part of the inheritance bequeathed to us by our
Lord; and it is one of the marks of a real Christian, and
of a true church. Where it is not found, the vital power
of Christianity is not enjoyed.

As such inquiries as those which are now under consideration are not unfrequently instituted, it is cause of
devout thankfulness to Almighty God, that the annals of
the Society supply ample materials for furnishing a most
satisfactory reply to them. Instead of entering, in support of this statement, with unnecessary minuteness of
detail, into an examination of the numerous and signal
proofs of the divine approbation connected with the proceedings of the Society, it will be sufficient for our present
purpose, to fix upon and compare two different periods in
its history, as, by so doing, all the information necessary,
in order to a clear understanding of the case, will be
exhibited. Let the year 1815 be selected, and a comparison be instituted between the circumstances of the
Society at that time, and in the year 1840 ; and we shall
at once perceive, that this cause, which originated like a
speck on the horizon, and the increase of which, at the
commencement, was so slow, has spread into a large
cloud, fraught with the richest blessings, which it is communicating to multitudes of people at the very ends of the
earth. These two periods are chosen, in preference to
others, because, about the year 1815, measures, rendered
necessary by the death of Dr. Coke, were adopted, under
the guidance of Divine Providence, which led to a more
complete and efficient organization of the Missionary
operations of the Connexion ; and in the year 1840, the
financial difficulties of the Society were most severely felt
by the Committee.

At the earlier period, the Society employed two Missionaries in Europe, who had under their care sixty-six members, or communicants; at the latter era, these had increased to about twenty-five Missionaries, (who occupied fourteen principal Stations,) and eighteen hundred and fourteen members.

The year 1815 witnessed the beginning of the labours of the Missionaries in Asia, that strong-hold of idolatry :—The Society in 1840 occupied twenty-one principal Stations in that quarter of the globe, with twenty-two Missionaries and seventeen Assistant-Missionaries, who had under their care twelve hundred and forty-three members, or communicants; in addition to which, inestimable benefits have been conferred upon thousands of the native population, by the Missionary schools and presses which have been, and still are, in active and efficient operation.

There were in the West Indies, exclusive of Jamaica, thirty-one Missionaries employed by the Society, in the year 1815, and upwards of fifteen thousand members in church-fellowship :—The number of Missionaries in 1840 was forty-eight, and of members, twenty-four thousand seven hundred and eighty-four. Still more rapid and extensive has been the progress of the work of God on the island of Jamaica, between the two periods which we are now comparing, and to which a more particular reference will be afterwards made.

In Africa, the fatherland of the black and coloured population of the West Indies, there were, under the care of the Society, in the southern and western sections of that continent, in 1815, only TWO Missionaries, who had one hundred and forty-two members under their pastoral care and direction :—But in 1840, the principal Stations amounted to forty-eight; the number of Missionaries and Assistants, to fifty-two; of salaried Teachers, to fifty-four; of church-members, to four thousand seven hundred and ninety-six : and of children attending the schools, to upwards of five thousand.

Throughout those immense and distant regions included under the general names of Australasia and Polynesia, the Society employed only ONE Missionary in 1815; at which

period no converts to the faith of Christ appeared in connexion with that (then) infant Mission. How greatly has
the state of things since changed for the better ! In New
South Wales, Australia Felix, and Van-Diemen's Land, the
Society occupies eleven principal Stations ; and in Southern
and Western Australia, two. The evangelical leaven has
been extensively diffused amongst the Aborigines of New-
Zealand. The Friendly Islanders have taken the yoke of
Christ upon them, and are learning of Him to be "meek and
lowly in heart." The cross has been successfully planted
on the dark and blood-stained shores of Feejee; while
other islands of the Pacific are waiting and looking for the
evangelical law. Instead of ONE Missionary in the Southern Hemisphere, there are now FORTY-SEVEN, and sixteen
salaried Teachers ; and in a part of the world in which the
Society had NOT A SINGLE MEMBER in 1815, there were
nearly ELEVEN THOUSAND in 1840, the greater number of
whom, a few brief years since, were under the dominion
of some of the lowest and most degrading forms of idolatry. Christian Schoolmasters are also abroad, who are
placing the elements of useful learning upon a religious
basis, in the minds of ten thousand nine hundred and
forty-six adults and children, belonging to the schools
connected with those Missions ; many of whom are converted Heathens, far advanced in years, but who are
sedulously learning to read the " oracles of God."

On that part of the continent of North America subject to
the British Crown, and on the neighbouring islands, thirty-
four Missionaries were stationed in 1815, who ministered
the word of life in those vast countries to a small and
widely-scattered population :—Ninety-three Missionaries
were engaged in that department of the work in 1840 ;
and the number of church-members had increased from
eighteen hundred and twenty-four, to eleven thousand six
hundred and eighty-one. In the judgment of an individual who filled the highest office in Newfoundland, that
colony is mainly indebted, for the degree of Protestant
influence which exists in it, to the labours of Wesleyan
Missionaries.

XIII.

Let the range of observation and comparison be now limited to two Districts,—that of South Ceylon and Jamaica, the one belonging to Asia, and the other to America. It has been already stated, that the inchoative operations of the Society in Asia may be dated from the year 1815. At that period there was a lamentable deficiency of Christian instruction in South Ceylon, as well as in every other part of the island; in consequence of which, the state of religion and of morals was very low, even amongst that portion of the inhabitants generally who made a profession of the Christian faith. Some provision was made at Colombo, as well as at one or two other places, for the spiritual instruction of the civil and military servants of the Crown; and the Government Chaplain was an ornament to his profession, and a blessing to the circle in which he moved. But, generally speaking, there was " a famine, not of bread," indeed, but of " the word of the Lord." On the arrival of the Missionaries, they found almost all that large portion of the inhabitants by whom the Indo-Portuguese language is spoken, " as sheep having no shepherd;" there being only one Minister of the Dutch Reformed Church, at head-quarters, provided for them, who preached in a language little understood by the male, and entirely unknown to the female, part of his congregation. The dominion of Heathenism over the Singhalese was unbroken and almost unquestioned; and the Priests, pointing to their crowded temples, laughed to scorn the messengers of truth.

Successive regiments of British troops have since been stationed on the island; in each of which, to quote the language of the soldiers themselves, some of them have had reason, on their departure from it, to say, " I was born and reared in Britain, a land of light, where I lived in darkness; and in Ceylon, a land of darkness, I have been made a partaker of the light of life." In not a few instances, these military converts were removed to Stations on the continent of India, and other places, where there were no Missionaries; in which, by their conversa-

tion and conduct, they shone as lights in the midst of
surrounding darkness, and, instrumentally, guided the feet
of even some of the natives, as well as of their comrades,
into the way of peace.* Moved with compassion for the
thousands of the people who spoke Indo-Portuguese, the
agents of the Society studied that dialect, and soon began
to convey religious instruction to them in their own
tongue. These services were numerously attended ; a
divine blessing accompanied the word ; congregations
have since been gathered ; chapels have been erected ;
men and women have been brought to a knowledge of the
truth ; and Christian societies have been organized, especially at Colombo, Galle, and Jaffna : and it is worthy of
notice, that the Assistant-Missionaries, whose number, in
1840, amounted to seven, have chiefly been raised up by
the blessing of God on this department of the work.
While occupied with these important and pressing duties,
the Missionaries appointed to Ceylon have never overlooked the paramount claims of the atheistical and
superstitious Aborigines on their sympathies and services. To meet their case, the Gospel is preached in
Singhalese ; books are printed and distributed ; and about
seventy schools are organized on exclusively religious
principles, which are attended by between four and five
thousand children. The conditions on which these schools
have been established afford a striking proof of the growing
strength of Christian influence amongst the natives ; for,
in addition to other stipulations, it is required, that the
inhabitants of the villages into which schools are introduced, shall build and keep in repair, at their own
expense, the house in which the children are taught ;
that the Teachers shall be selected by the Missionaries ;
and that no heathen books shall be used in any of the
schools under any pretence whatever. In these semi-
naries, the influence of caste, which formerly occasioned

* One of the most useful Assistant-Missionaries in the island of Ceylon in the service of the Society, was brought to a knowledge of the
truth, and converted to the faith of Christ, by means of one of the pious
soldiers, who had himself been the fruit of Missionary labour in that
island.

so much difficulty to the Missionaries, is now utterly subdued; and the children are classified according to their
ability and attainments, without reference to their social
rank. The schools themselves supply an adequate number of suitable Instructors; some of whom are not only
qualified to teach the rising generation, but to explain and
enforce the impressive truths of the Gospel among their
parents; a duty which they gladly discharge on the day
of the Lord, in the same places in which the children are
instructed on the ordinary days of the week. It will be
readily admitted, that these are great advantages; and
when it is considered, that the entire canon of holy Scrip-
ture is now circulated amongst the Singhalese, and amongst
the descendants of the former European possessors of that
island, in the two languages spoken by them; that both
these translations were greatly promoted by our Missionaries, and were printed for the Colombo Auxiliary Bible
Society, at the press sent out by the Wesleyan Missionary
Society; who can refuse to recognise, in such results,
cause of devout gratitude for the past, and of hope for the
future? The standard of Christian feeling and practice
has been elevated amongst professing Christians; a native
ministry is growing up; the schools are providing Teachers
and Catechists; and scriptural truth is disseminated by the
Missionary, the Schoolmaster, and the Press. By the blessing of God on these means, which other Societies are employing there, as well as our own, a blow has been inflicted
on the .power of the Prince of darkness in that lovely
region, from the effect of which it will never recover; for,
in the judgment of an individual whose opinion on such
a subject is entitled to the highest respect, Christianity
has struck its roots so firmly into the moral soil of Ceylon, that, if every European Missionary were to be with-
drawn from that country, it would still live, and flourish,
and bring forth fruit to the praise and glory of God.
Already there is " a noise and a shaking" in the valley in
which the messengers of the Lord prophesied twenty-five
years ago, and said, " O ye dry bones, hear the word of
the Lord." As the voice shall continue to sound, the
" sinews and the flesh" will come upon them, and " the

skin will cover them" above; until, at length, the breath of the Holy Spirit shall touch and revivify the dead. Nor is it unreasonable to hope, that, from Ceylon, the word of the Lord will go forth to Burma and China, in which the principles of Budhism prevail so extensively; and that the desire of receiving some signal good from that "sacred isle," which has been long cherished by the teeming population of those great empires, will be accomplished in a manner very different from their present wishes and expectations.

Turning from the east to the west, the progress of the work in Jamaica may be traced, during the same period. It will be recollected, that, in the year 1815, the motives and proceedings of the Missionaries in that island were viewed with suspicion and distrust, by a large and influential portion of the inhabitants; and that the Missionaries themselves were treated with much personal and official disrespect and indignity. On some occasions, popular fury was let loose, and directed against them, in defiance of the law; and, on others, legal forms and technicalities were employed, by their powerful and misguided adversaries, as the covering for acts of oppression and injustice. In Kingston, the Wesleyan Missionaries were prevented from preaching the Gospel, by the municipal authorities; and in many other places the same hostile spirit was frequently manifested. All the agents of the Society then in the colony were placed in circumstances of great trial and difficulty; and some of them even suffered "bonds and imprisonment, for the sake of the Lord Jesus." That was a day of small things, of gloom and of darkness, in the history of the Jamaica Mission.

With Ministers silenced, societies scattered, chapels closed, and surrounded by numerous, active, and determined foes, the members of society cried to the Lord for help; and most instructive, as well as touching, is the recorded account of the proceedings of a portion of the flock, at the time when Mr. Davies applied to the proper quarter, for permission to exercise his ministry amongst them. A few days before the one selected by the members of the tribunal to which the Missionary had appealed, for consider-

ing and deciding on his case, the pious people held a day
of solemn fasting and prayer, " to entreat the Lord to look
upon the afflicted state of the church in Jamaica, and par-
ticularly in Kingston," where the house of God had been
shut nearly seven years; and, of course, so long had the
public ministry of the word been suspended.   The desired
permission was obtained, and the chapel was immediately
repaired and re-opened for public worship, to the inexpressible joy of multitudes.   They were, however, soon
called to endure a new trial of their faith, in the sudden
death of their beloved Pastor; when the sanctuary was
again closed, no other Missionary being licensed by the
magistracy of the place.   But in the midst of these discouraging circumstances, their language was, " We must
not despair: if we put our trust in the Lord, and call upon
Him, we may reasonably hope for ultimate success."   Nor
did they hope in vain.   That day has passed away, never,
we believe, to return.   Attention is now directed to these
painful occurrences, not for the purpose of reviving the
recollection of events upon which all parties look back
with regret, but that a deeper impression may be made
with respect to the altered circumstances in which the
Mission is now placed, and that thanksgivings to Almighty
God may be called forth, on account of the greatly improved state of things in that important colony.   Men of
all ranks, and of various religious persuasions, approve of
and encourage the Missionaries in their unwearied endeavours to instruct the peasantry.   Public aid has been
afforded, and private liberality has been and is largely
exercised, by magistrates, planters, and other influential
persons, in support of the Mission, the design and tendency of which are now properly understood, and duly
appreciated: so that, looking at the present tranquil and
flourishing—as compared with the former disturbed and
depressed—state of the Wesleyan community in Jamaica,
the description which is given of the churches throughout
all Judea, and Galilee, and Samaria, may with great pro-
priety be applied to its members; for they have " rest,"
and are " edified;" and, " walking in the fear of the Lord,
and in the comfort of the Holy Ghost, are multiplied."

In the Minutes of Conference for the year 1815, the entire island of Jamaica comprised but one Circuit; in 1840, it was divided into eighteen. Between the two periods which are under review, the Missionaries have increased from four to twenty-nine; to which number should be added, as belonging to the same District, one at the Grand Caymanas, and two at Belize and Charibb-Town, Honduras-Bay: while, within the same time, the number in church-fellowship, which, in 1815, amounted to two thousand seven hundred, now exceeds twenty-three thousand. It will be seen, from an examination of the official documents, on the authority of which these statements are made, that, in the year 1840, a larger number of Missionaries were stationed in Kingston alone, than were on the whole island twenty-five years before that time; and a larger number of members in the colony, in 1840, by upwards of FIVE THOUSAND, than there were IN ALL THE WEST-INDIA ISLANDS, INCLUDING JAMAICA, occupied by the Society in the year 1815. What hath God wrought?

The result of this whole comparison shows, that, in connexion with the Wesleyan Missions in Europe, Asia, Africa, America, Australasia, and Polynesia, between the years 1815 and 1840, that is to say, during the comparatively short interval of twenty-five years, the number of Missionaries had increased from seventy-four to about three hundred and sixty-seven, and to nearly an equal number of salaried Teachers; and the members, in communion with that portion of the great Christian family, from nineteen thousand three hundred and eighty-five, to about eighty thousand. Assuming,—what, under the circumstances, may be regarded as a moderate estimate,—that three times the number of persons recognised as communicants attend the ministry of the Missionaries, then it will appear, that, while in 1815 less than sixty thousand individuals heard the Gospel preached by Wesleyan Missionaries, the number in 1840 had increased to nearly a quarter of a million, a large portion of whom are as lights shining in the dark places of the earth, which are yet, to an awful extent, filled with "the habitations of cruelty."

XIV.

THIS review of the progress of the Missions, encouraging as it is, by no means embraces all those elements which should enter into our calculations, if we would form just conceptions of the success with which God has been pleased to reward the exertions of the Society. Other considerations, connected with this topic, still remain to be examined.

When an estimate is made of the number of persons living in a state of peace and order, under the spiritual care of the Missionaries, for the purpose of forming a judgment of the amount of good which has been realized by their instrumentality, the former state and character of the converts which have been made should be taken into consideration. The "messengers of the churches," who have been sent into heathen lands, did not, on their arrival, generally find a people, in any considerable measure, prepared by education, habit, or prejudice, for the reception of the truths which they were commissioned to announce in the name of the Lord; but, on the contrary, a state of things usually as different from that as can well be conceived, and one in which all these were arrayed against the Teacher and his doctrines. Ministers who deliver the message of salvation in this country, have, to a great extent, on the side of truth, the influence belonging to early impressions and recollections; all that is deemed respectable in example and station; the weight of public opinion and profession; the force of national feelings and predilections, and, not unfrequently, of personal convictions, and of domestic associations. These, with the far greater proportion of his audience, are in favour of the Preacher. He and his hearers hold many of those principles in common upon which he founds and enforces the reasonings and exhortations that he addresses to the judgment and to the conscience. If, with all these and other important advantages connected with the exercise of the Christian ministry at home, the progress of true religion and virtue is so slow amongst the people; and if the number is comparatively so small, who, like the primitive Christians in Jerusalem, continue " steadfastly in the Apostles' doctrine and fellowship, and in breaking of bread, and in prayers ; " the friends of foreign Missions may well " thank God, and take courage," on account of their numerical increase, as well as of the other signs of progressive improvement which they present to the view of every unprejudiced observer.

Amongst the thousands who are receiving instruction from the Missionaries, there are many who were once under the dominion of debasing and degrading systems of error and wickedness, to which they nevertheless adhered with great tenacity, and around which the strongest feelings of our common nature were entwined ;— persons whose views of the Supreme Being were not elevated beyond the rude and mis-shapen figure of wood or of stone, before which they bowed themselves, and said, " It is a god ; " whose religious services were not only adapted to their cruel and depraved tastes and propensities, but added to their terrible energy ; whose intellect was wholly uncultivated ; whose very affections were unnatural, and prompted them to torment and destroy the living, that they might honour and gratify the dead ; who had lost all power of discerning between moral good and evil, and seemed to have reached the lowest point to which human nature can sink in the present world ; being " full of envy, murder, debate, deceit, malignity." Such was the state of a part of the human quarry into which the Missionaries penetrated ; and out of that portion of it they have brought many of the " living stones" which they, as the instruments of the Holy Spirit, have hewn, and polished, and placed upon the " foundation of the Apostles and Prophets, Jesus Christ himself being the chief corner-stone." Indeed, so utterly hopeless did the condition of some of the objects of Missionary benevolence appear to be, that the very attempt to improve their condition awakened the pity of a few, and excited the contempt of many, for those who engaged in such a task themselves, or encouraged others : now, therefore, after the experiment has been tried, and has succeeded, the very manner in which it was once opposed shows the magnitude of the difficulties which had to be encountered, and enhances the value of the success which has attended the undertaking.

There is another aspect under which this part of the case should be regarded. Believing that the general spread of the Gospel throughout the world is closely connected with *the re-establishment of the dominion of scriptural truth,* and *the revival of spiritual religion, in all the continental Protestant Churches,* the proceedings of the Wesleyan Missionary Society in different European countries are conducted with a special reference to these objects. This is a truly Christian design, and perfectly accords with the generous spirit and object of the man whom God employed as the great Founder of Methodism. It is an attempt to strengthen the interests of the Redeemer's kingdom within the boundaries of Christendom, rather than to increase the power of a particular class of Christians ; to win souls to the Saviour, rather than to make sectarian proselytes ; to promote union and co-operation amongst the adherents of the " one faith," instead of increasing the causes of difference and dissension which are everywhere too numerous. This part of the Society's plan may be, and is, carried out with great success in places where the persons are few in number who are formally and professedly united with the Church, under the immediate pastoral care of the Missionary. Such is the case of the Mission at Stockholm. Looking at that Station in a numerical point of view only, it would appear as if the services of the Missionary are there unproductive, and might elsewhere be more beneficially employed ; and yet such a conclusion would be most unjust and erroneous, since it would be difficult to find a place where a single agent of the Society possesses and exercises such an amount of religious influence, or is doing so much to maintain and spread scriptural godliness, as Mr. Scott, the Society's representative in Sweden. By a combination of providential circumstances, that Missionary occupies a place of singular usefulness ; and is indirectly contributing in various ways, to the revival and spread of a living and powerful spirit of religion in the national Church, as well as to defeat the efforts of the

Romish agents in that part of Northern Europe. The pure and beneficial design and tendency of his labours are, there is reason to believe, duly appreciated by influential individuals, who, for his work's sake, afford him their valuable protection and encouragement; and the fears which he has inspired in the mind of the Pope's Vicar-Apostolic, are thus stated, in a communication which appeared some months ago in one of the numbers of the " Annals of Catholicism in Europe : "—

" On the other hand, although there are no Methodists in Sweden, the Methodist Society of London has sent funds for the erection of a church, according to its worship, at Stockholm : they do not confine their sacrifices to that; and the Vicar-Apostolic fears, that in his flock, a prey to misery and neglect, a Society which disposes of so many means may bring about many defections."

Much and justly as we are attached to our distinctive rites and usages, we still possess such a measure of the original and best peculiarity of our system,—*a simple and paramount desire to spread scriptural holiness at home and abroad*,—as will lead us to rejoice when good is done in any country, by the instrumentality of Methodism, though not always under its particular name and forms.

It would be equally unsafe to judge, by a numerical rule, of the progress of our Missions in other countries which differ not less widely from Sweden in their geographical position, than they do in many other respects : for example, the interior Stations in South Africa. In several of those remote establishments, few indeed in number are the persons that have attained to such a degree of spiritual knowledge, or understanding in the things of God, as qualifies them for early admission into a state of Christian communion and church-membership. But, even in those parts in which the fewest number of men have been progressively gathered into the fold of Christ by the preaching of the Gospel, much evil is prevented, and much good is done, by the presence and labours of the Missionary amongst the rude people with whom he dwells. Is it not cause of rejoicing, that the glorious doctrines of the cross are thus made known to thousands of human beings, in their scriptural character and relations, in the freeness and fulness of their import, as well as in their prevailing influence and saving effects, as seen in the devout conduct and chaste conversation of their converted countrymen? Is it not of importance that a faithful and perpetual testimony is borne, by this gradually accumulating nucleus of a Christian church, against murder, polygamy, theft, witchcraft, and all the other evils to which the people have been so long addicted? Is it not a vast public benefit that some of the tribes are prevented from plunging into fierce and destructive conflicts with each other? that the ordinances of religion are established at each Mission Station, around which many of the heathen families are collected and reside, on the express condition, that they shall attend public worship, and that the children shall be sent to the Mission school? In places where the number of persons professing the Christian faith is inconsiderable, an influence in favour of Christianity has by these means been created, which is daily increasing; and, as has been justly remarked by a writer on the spot, " the salvation of many individuals from the frightful gulf of heathenish abominations, and the diffusion of light and truth through whole communities of immortal men, are no mean achievements, as the annals of eternity will clearly show." The civilizing tendency of the principles and institutions of the Gospel is gradually developing itself, in connexion with the Missions in that part of Africa, as well as in other places. Schools are established. Portions of the Sacred Volume, and of other useful books, have been translated and printed, and are circulated amongst the people; many of whom, of different classes and ages, have learned to read them, and a much greater number are engaged in learning. A periodical is published in the Kaffer language, and obtains numerous readers in places where, a few years since, the people were wholly ignorant of the existence of letters. The character of their wars has been affected by the influence of Missionary instruction; and the more recent conflicts that have taken place are not marked with those deeds of unsparing cruelty and horror which were formerly perpetrated by them in their hostile encounters with each other, or when they contended against a common foe. And, last, though not least, as a sign of social advancement, trade is following in the path of the Minister of the God of peace; and British manufactured goods of various descriptions, to the amount of several thousand pounds annually, are now carried over the colonial frontier, into a country where the fruits of the skill and industry of England were unknown, until the Missionary prepared the way for their introduction. When will England learn, from this and other facts connected with modern Missions, that, by devoting her vast resources to the honour of God, by promoting the spread of the Gospel of his Son amongst all nations, she will most effectually increase and perpetuate the sources of her commercial wealth and greatness?

In connexion with these tokens for good which this Mission presents, it will be found, on examination, that the work of spiritual conversion has been accomplished, in not a few instances, by the instrumentality of " the word of truth;" and as it is in the nature of genuine Christianity to diffuse itself, the converts whom it has already made among Kaffers, and Sichuanas, and Griquas, and other tribes, will be witnesses for the truth amongst their fellows; and by the evidence of its transforming energy which their spirit and conduct afford, as well as by their exhortations, the number of the faithful will be multiplied. Thaba Unchu, Umpukani, and 'Mparane have been recently visited by a gracious effusion of the Holy Spirit, which has been productive of the happiest results. One of the natives who shared in the blessedness of this visitation has since died, in sure and certain hope of a glorious resurrection unto eternal life; exclaiming, with almost his latest breath : " O Lord, my heavenly Father, come and take home thy child!"

To the benefits which Kafferland has derived from the zealous and judicious services of the Wesleyan Missionaries, a strong and honourable testimony is borne in the publication of Mr. Steedman, an intelligent and impartial witness, who visited that part of Africa in the prosecution of scientific inquiries and objects. The impression which his favourable representations of the state of the Missions made upon the mind of Lord Viscount Gage, led that Nobleman to address a communication to the Secretaries of the Parent Society, requesting permission to contribute what his Lordship was pleased to call his "mite" towards so good a work, and containing the following, amongst other truly valuable, sentiments :—

"As it may be interesting to your Society to know how a member of the Established Church, and an adherent specially of that portion of it generally considered least favourable to Missions, has been induced to make this application to you, I beg to state, distinctly and unequivocally, that it is the result of conviction of the well-directed zeal and actual utility of your Missions in South Africa, gathered from facts recorded in the Journal of a Naturalist, of the name of Steedman. A disinterested and unprejudiced eye-witness has given evidence of what he himself has seen in operation; and, in my mind, his account leaves no longer room for two opinions upon the question of—whether Missions, conducted as yours have been, are or are not really useful in a country circumstanced as South Africa now is.

"Zeal in Missionaries it were hardly reasonable to doubt; but when we have evidence, bearing internal marks of truth, that this zeal, under the direction of any given Society, has universally, throughout a large District, embracing many Stations, and under varied and trying circumstances, been tempered by reason, sober discretion, and that true courage in difficulties which genuine piety alone can give; and when we see the good fruit come, as the natural result of the conduct which, under the divine blessing, has produced it; I consider the problem as solved, the grand desideratum attained, and that the coldest amongst us can scarcely do otherwise than admit that this is a thing which, as a Christian, it has become his duty to support.

"Most sincerely do I pray, that many of my fellows may view the matter in this light, now especially when steady co-operation has been rendered so desirable by the losses recently incurred in the Kaffer war; and that those who, like myself, might not entirely agree with you in the wording of an abstract of Christianity, will merge all fancied differences in the consideration, that these things have little or nothing to do with the conversion of savages; and, moreover, that it will not unfrequently happen, that forms, really the most eligible for more mature stages of society, may nevertheless be found perhaps the very least adapted to its infancy."

XV.

THERE are other evidences of the progress of the Missions of a very important character which yet remain to be considered, and which it will be proper here to notice.

At the commencement of the year 1815, the Missionaries,

with one or two exceptions, preached the Gospel in the
English language only; in 1840 they and their Assistants
communicated religious instruction in Swedish, in French,
in German, and in Spanish, on the Continent of Europe;
in Tamul, Canarese, Portuguese, Singhalese, and occasionally in Teloogoo, Pali, and Dutch, in different parts of
Asia; in Kaffer, Sichuana, Dutch, Namacqua, Jolloof,
Mandingo, Fantee, and other dialects of Africa; in
Ojibewa, French, and Spanish, in America, including the
West Indies; and in the languages of New-Zealand, the
Friendly Islands, and Feejee, in the Southern Hemisphere. Through the medium of these various forms of
speech and language, the Agents of the Society are saying
to perishing men, "Behold the Lamb of God which
taketh away the sin of the world!" At the former
period, the labours of the Missionaries were limited to a
portion of the foreign possessions of the Crown; now
" their sound " has gone into all the colonial provinces of
the empire; and also into " the regions beyond," where
the British flag is not recognised, except when once a
week it is unfurled at the Mission Station, as the " outward and visible sign " of the return of that day which the
Lord hath blessed and hallowed. Then, the Society employed no presses on any one of the Mission Stations;
now it possesses seven printing establishments;—two in
Southern Africa, one in Ceylon, and another on the Continent of India, one in New-Zealand, one at the Friendly
Islands, and one in Feejee. The Scholastic efforts of the
Society which were just beginning in the year 1815, have
since been greatly enlarged; so much so, that in 1840 the
Schools were attended by nearly fifty-seven thousand
pupils. Then there were no Auxiliary Missionary Societies abroad, co-operating with the Parent Society in its
endeavours to evangelize all nations; now there is one
connected with every Foreign District. In 1815, no
money was raised on the Foreign Stations for general
Missionary purposes; while, in 1840, the Contributions to
the Parent Society from abroad amounted to about eleven
thousand pounds. The Indian and the Kaffer, the New-
Zealander and the Hottentot, are learning to practise

the Christian precept: " Freely ye have received, freely give."

These are encouraging manifestations of the presence of God with his servants, in the work to which he has called them.

"Sons of God, your Saviour praise,
HE the door hath open'd wide ;
Jesus gives the word of grace,
Jesu's word is glorified."

During the last twenty-five years, the boundaries of the church have been extended, and new centres of operation have been formed in many of the strong-holds of error and superstition, from which the light and influence of the Gospel are going forth in every direction ; and renovating agencies are now in successful operation in regions where sin and misery, under their worst aspects, exercised undisputed sway. A great preparatory work has been accomplished in various places. Obstinate prejudices have been removed. The Missionaries, by their prudent and disinterested behaviour, have established a character for themselves, that gives immense influence to the cause in which they are engaged. Barbarous languages have been reduced to a written form ; and, in consequence of that, future Missionaries will be enabled to acquire a knowledge of them at a comparatively small expenditure of time and labour. The word of God, in whole or in part, the Catechisms for youth, prepared and published under the direction and sanction of the Conference, together with numerous other useful publications, have been translated into the languages used by the Agents of the Society, and have been widely circulated. Few though the number of converts be to the Christian faith from amongst the idolatrous population in our Anglo-Indian empire, connected with the Wesleyan and other Protestant Missions, yet there are not wanting unequivocal indications of the approach of a brighter day in the East. Splendid and durable as those idolatrous systems seem to be, which so long have led captive the teeming population of Hindostan, there are many under-currents, flowing in various directions ; these, though almost unnoticed, are washing away the very foundations on which the idolatry of India is based, together with the entire " refuge of lies," within which it has found a shelter and a defence.

A spirit of Christian zeal and liberality is developing itself on the foreign Stations, which is already felt to be most beneficial in its operation.   This is a natural fruit of the love of God shed abroad in the heart of the Christian believer, in whatever clime he may reside.   It is one of the modes by which the " new affection " every where displays itself, and is inseparable from a sound state of religious experience and enjoyment.   The same constraining motive which prompted the members of the Connexion at home to send the glad tidings of salvation abroad, is now acting upon those new converts ; and, under its influence, they are making efforts to perpetuate Christian ordinances amongst themselves, as well as to send them into countries where the Saviour is not yet known, " that all men may see what is the fellowship of the mystery, which from the beginning of the world hath been hid in God, who created all things by Christ Jesus."   The power of this principle amongst the societies abroad is manifested in the fervour of their prayers for the deliverance of others from that state of misery from which they themselves have been rescued ; in the erection of Chapels and School-houses ; in the formation of Associations for religious and charitable objects ; in the cheerfulness with which they contribute a portion of the little they possess, to assist in supporting those who preach the Gospel to them, and also for the purpose of promoting the great objects of the Parent Society.   It should be here stated, to the glory of God, who by his grace has called the members of our Missionary churches to be his " sons and daughters," and, by so doing, has made them willing to be his " servants," that—in addition to between ten and eleven thousand pounds contributed by them, and remitted to the Treasurers, to be expended under the direction of the General Committee—upwards of thirty thousand pounds are raised annually in the Missionary Districts towards the maintenance of the Missionaries, who debit themselves with such a portion of this total sum as may have been received by each respectively during the year, and draw for so much less of the amount of allowances to which they are entitled on the general fund at home.* In this way the older Stations are doing as much as they can to lighten the financial burdens of the Society : And that they will do more, in proportion as their circumstances improve, may be safely inferred from what they have already done ; for, taking number for number, it will be seen that they are not surpassed by the members under the care of any other Missionary Institution, in the extent of their contributions, and that in few instances, if in any, are they equalled in this branch of duty. So great were the exertions which were made in the West Indies in the year 1840, to lighten the pressure on the funds at home, that those Missions cost about Six Thousand Pounds less to the Society, than the sum which was expended upon them in the course of the preceding year. Within the same period, the Societies in the Demarara District not only provided for the support of their own Missionaries, but repaid to the General Treasurers four hundred and fifty pounds, which had been advanced some years before for the relief of one of the Chapels in that colony; and, in addition, sent home upwards of a thousand Pounds, the proceeds of their Auxiliary Missionary Society.

Nor, in estimating the result of Missionary exertions, should the fact be overlooked, that they are identified with eternity. It is indeed a delightful employment to the Christian, in whose heart dwells an ardent and zealous

---

* The aid thus afforded is of great importance, not only in a financial point of view, but as a proof of the high sense which is entertained of the beneficial effects of the labours of the Missionaries in those very places where they are stationed. These moneys are contributed by all classes of persons ; many of whom fill the highest stations in the countries in which they reside, and have excellent opportunities for judging correctly of the character and proceedings of the agents of the Society abroad. This is a practical answer, of the most satisfactory kind, to the insinuations which are sometimes hazarded by persons in this country unfriendly to Missions,—that the Missionaries are doing no good; that they are indolent, selfish, and useless ! Why, then, do Governors, Judges, Magistrates, Merchants, and others, on the spot, who observe the men and their communications daily, contribute liberally towards their support ?

desire that "the unsearchable riches of Christ may be made known to the Gentiles," to range over Missionary Stations, and to contemplate the trophies of grace with which they are adorned. But if justice is to be done to the lofty theme, he must, by faith, pass beyond the veil which divides the Church militant on earth from the Church triumphant in heaven; and look upon the goodly number there, who, having from our own and other Mission Stations, passed through death to their eternal home, are now before the Throne, the first-fruits to God, and to the Lamb, of the various countries of which they are the glorified representatives.

XVI.

Such is the view which the present, as compared with the former, state of the Wesleyan Missions furnishes to the inquirer; and it is surely most encouraging. Here is an answer both to the sneers of the heartless infidelity of the world at this undertaking, and to the bigotry and exclusiveness which prevail in some portions of the church. Men who are nourished by the bounty of Protestantism,—and yet either protest against the great principles of the Reformation, or practically contradict them; who themselves appeal to no proofs that they are commissioned to preach the Gospel but such as it is more difficult to find, than it is to discover grass and flowers amidst the arid sands of an African desert,—decry as "unauthorized teachers and presumptuous intruders into the sacred office" those whom it hath pleased God to honour, by having employed them in the accomplishment of this great work. The character and the usefulness of the men triumphantly refute the accusatory statements of their haughty assailants. Missionaries who preach "the Apostles' doctrine," who have imbibed the apostolic spirit, who endure apostolic hardships and privations, who share in apostolic success, must be in the true Christian "apostolic succession." In the sense in which Rome employs that term, and by means of which she makes merchandise of the souls of men, her imitators and advocates shall, as far as the Wesleyan Methodists are concerned, enjoy the sole and undisputed possession of it. Instead of seeking, in the purlieus of the seat of the papacy, for evidence of their claim to the character of ambassadors of Christ, Wesleyan Ministers will themselves obey "the sure word," and exhort others to take heed to it, which says, " Come out of her, my people, that ye be not partakers of her sins, and that ye receive not of her plagues." How can she bless, who, because she preaches another Gospel, is herself under an anathema? Or how can she give authority to Ministers of Christ, who is, preeminently and emphatically, an antichrist? The Wesleyan Missionaries—having been "inwardly moved by the Holy Ghost" to enter upon their sacred vocation; and, after due examination of the reality of that call, (as far as man can judge on such a subject,) set apart to their office and work by the imposition of the hands and prayers "of the Presbytery"—went forth " in weakness and in fear," but fully persuaded that they were called to " teach" God's holy word, and to administer his holy sacraments " in the congregation." The fruit of their labours proves that they were not mistaken, and that God has through them made known the savour of his grace in the places which they have visited. It is, no doubt, very convenient for intolerant and exclusive Ecclesiastics, who can produce no such corroborative testimony of the vocation which they profess to have received to be " ambassadors for Christ," to question or deny the validity of attesting evidence of this description; and to substitute for " living epistles, known and read of all men," an invisible and intangible line, connecting—strange extremes!—the APOSTLES and THEMSELVES. But we appeal from the tribunal of such judges as these to the highest authority on this subject, even to that of " the Lord of all," who, when the disciples of John inquired of him, on behalf of their master, " Art thou He that should come, or do we look for another?" said unto them, " Go, and show John again those things which ye do hear and see,—the blind receive their sight, the lepers are cleansed, and the deaf hear, the dead are raised up, and the poor have the Gospel preached to them." It is admitted, that the two cases are not identical; nor is it necessary to our argument

that they should be, inasmuch as the principle here maintained is not that of identity, but of analogy. The question propounded by the agents of John was, in reality,
" Art thou the Messiah ? " The Saviour replied to it, by
pointing to his works; of which he said on another occasion, " They bear witness of me, that I am he." What
we maintain is, that we are justified, by the example of
the Great Teacher, in appealing to the effects which
accompany and follow the ministrations of our Missionaries, in proof of the reality of their vocation to " preach
the word," and to gather and " to feed the flock of Christ
which he hath bought with his blood." Let the call to
the pastoral office, which they profess to have received, be
tried by the principle involved in the test to which our
Lord referred,—let them be judged by " their fruits,"—
and we have no fear for the issue ; for it will be seen,
that the spiritual and moral effects which, according to
the sacred oracles, prove the presence of Christ with his
Ministers, are produced by the instrumentality of the
Missionaries ; and that now, as in the first days of Christianity, " the word " is " confirmed by " those " signs "
which always follow the preaching of the Gospel, when it
comes " not in word only, but in power, in the Holy
Ghost, and in much assurance." Were men " pricked to
the heart " while primitive Evangelists exhorted them to
" flee from the wrath to come ? " This effect has been
produced in numerous instances, under the preaching of
the same doctrine, by our Missionaries, accompanied by
the same spiritual agency ; and godly sorrow is felt and
expressed by human beings, who never shed a tear until
they were led to weep for their sins. Were believers
" filled with all peace and joy through believing," in the
early days of the church? So are the converts on our
Mission Stations, at the present time ; as their artless and
scriptural statements testify. Were men then " turned
from dumb idols to serve the living God," by the power
of the Gospel? This result has been effected in our
day, amongst whole tribes and communities of men.
Were the early followers of the Lamb led to " walk in
love one towards another ? " The same lesson has been

successfully taught, by modern Missionaries, to their flocks; and those who breathed nothing but slaughter against each other, are now united together in bonds stronger than those of kindred or of patriotism,—in the bonds of Christian affection. Did apostolic converts triumph over sickness and death? So do those whom God has given to our Missionaries to be their " hope, and joy, and crown of rejoicing, in the day of the Lord Jesus." " Jesus Christ is my only foundation," and, " I am going to Jesus," constitute the sum and substance of their dying testimony.

XVII.

WE are directed by a primitive rule to judge of the claims of the evangelical ambassador, from the character of his embassy, and the fruits of his Mission. " Hear what St. John saith : " " If there come any unto you, and bring not this doctrine,"—the doctrine, that Christ is come in the flesh,—" receive him not into your house, neither bid him God speed ; for he that biddeth him God speed is partaker of his evil deeds." " Hear also what St. Paul saith : " " But though we," Paul himself, " or " even a more illustrious being,—" an angel from heaven, preach any other Gospel unto you than that which we have preached unto you,"—the doctrine, that men are justified by faith only,—" let him be accursed : " and the same sacred writer maintained his claim to the apostolic office, in opposition to the accusations and insinuations of his adversaries, by an appeal to his apostolic labours and success. Far be it from us to impugn Christian authority and order in the church of God. The Wesleyan Methodists are not ignorant of their necessity and value, when scripturally administered and enforced, for the purpose of maintaining and spreading Christian truth and purity. But if externalism is to be unduly magnified, or perverted to schismatical uses and purposes ; if forms and circumstances are to be substituted for the vitality, power, and charity of the Gospel ; if things doubtful are to be made as important as the faith by which cometh salvation ; if as much zeal is to be manifested in attempts to draw Missionaries from their present religious connexions, as in persuading heathen Priests to forsake their idolatrous altars, and to turn to the Saviour ; if Papal Rome is to be practically honoured, and the hand which is held up against laborious and useful Protestant Pastors, is to be offered as a token of friendship and fellowship to the accredited agents of error, and if an imaginary lineal succession is to secure for them proofs of official consideration and respect, which are denied to the faithful Ministers of truth ; if efforts are to be made to unsettle the minds of sincere and upright professors of Christianity, because they do not follow a particular form or method of worship, rather than to convert sinners from the error of their ways ; if the wheat, growing in that part of the field which Wesleyan labourers have cultivated, is to be called " darnel," because it is not enclosed within a particular fence, or does not grow on stalks of a certain size and form :—if these things are to be, then, while we shall bring no " railing accusations against others," nor abandon any one of those great principles which, " through good report and through evil report," we have asserted and upheld, we will endeavour to make it appear to all men, that we know how to distinguish between " things that differ," and to pursue " a more excellent way." Standing on " the pillar and ground of the truth," the Wesleyan Ministers abroad, as well as at home, pointing to their children in the Lord, with feelings of devout gratitude to the Author of all good, will still say, in reply to the ridiculous and arrogant claims of their traducers, " Are not we Ministers of Christ ? ' Are not' these our ' work in the Lord ? ' If we be not Ministers ' unto others, yet doubtless ' we are to these ; ' for the seals of our ministry ' are ' these in the Lord.' "

XVIII.

DURING the period which we have been comparing, many human schemes and enterprises have been projected, and have failed ; but this cause, " like a tree planted by the rivers of water," has been and still is fruitful and flourishing. Christian churches have been multiplied in heathen lands ; and the sanctifying energy of the Gospel has been diffused, and its principles estab-

lished, amongst communities once under the dominion of
Paganism. The song of holy praise is heard in places
which, not long ago, echoed only to the cries of savage
beasts, or still more savage men. Children's voices are
lifted up in the desert, lisping "their young Hosannas"
to the newly-discovered Saviour's name. Intelligence,
wonder, and joy beam in the tattooed countenance of the
once-untutored barbarian, as he meditates in " the Book "
that unfolds to him " things which the angels desire to
look into." Hostile Chiefs meet at the table of the Lord,
where they bury all their former animosities, and kneel
together as brethren. The joyful mother holds up her
living child, now devoted to God in baptism, and blesses
Him for the " unspeakable gift" of a religion which
spreads its shield over the innocence and helplessness of
infancy, and but for which that child would have been
devoted to demons and to destruction. Instead of sitting,
as the roving Indian used to do, in his heathen state, on
the margin of some river or lake in the wilderness, torn
with anguish, lest the child, of which death had deprived
him, should have been unsuccessful in his attempt to
cross the narrow strait which, according to Indian tradi-
tion, he would have to pass to the hunting-grounds in the
far West; now, (to use the language of the Chief Shawundais already referred to,) under similar visitations, he
"wipes the tears from his eye, while he reads," in his
own tongue, the consolatory language of our Lord to his
disciples : " Let not your heart be troubled ; ye believe in
God, believe also in me. In my Father's house are many
mansions; if it were not so, I would have told you. I
go to prepare a place for you. And if I go and prepare a
place for you, I will come again, and receive you unto
myself; that where I am, there ye may be also." Marks
of temporal amelioration, as well as of spiritual improvement, are associated with the scenes of Missionary success. The natives of New-Zealand are now seen sailing
to or from the house of God, and the vessels with which
they occasionally trade ; instead of plying their canoes up
and down the Hokianga, in search of their enemies, and
maintaining dreadful contests with each other. Habits of

sobriety and industry have been introduced amongst once
intemperate and wretched Indians; and at the St. Clair
Station the average annual number of deaths in the tribe
has been reduced, since they were brought under the
influence of the Gospel, from between thirty and forty to
less than five. These and similar triumphs, while they
admonish, also encourage us, by saying to all who, at
home or abroad, have contributed to produce them:
" Therefore be ye steadfast and unmovable, always
abounding in the work of the Lord; forasmuch as ye
know that your labour is not in vain in the Lord." For
" the deaf hear the words of the book, and the eyes of
the blind see out of obscurity, and out of darkness. The
meek increase their joy in the Lord, and the poor among
men rejoice in the Holy One of Israel."

XIX.

THEN this cause, identified as it is with the glory of
God and the best interests of man, and over which the
Lamb watches with untiring vigilance, must not be neglected or forsaken by " the bride, the Lamb's wife." She
must be up and doing, making herself ready for the coming of the Bridegroom. The members of the church have
great duties to perform, in order that the church may fulfil
her high destiny; and the question which here arises, and
requires a careful consideration, is, How shall the Wesleyan Methodists, as constituting a part of that church,
most effectually meet the obligations which have provi-
dentially devolved upon them, in connexion with the Missionary enterprise? They should enter upon this task, by
regarding the cause of the Redeemer in the world as a
solemn trust, which he has in part committed to them,
and which they are to defend, to maintain, and to extend,
with as much care and fidelity as if it were their own. It
is our joy and boast, that the salvation which is in Christ
Jesus becomes ours, when we believe " with the heart
unto righteousness." We gratefully acknowledge, that
believers " have redemption through his blood, the forgiveness of sins;" that they are " predestinated to the
adoption of children" by Christ Jesus; that they have
received, by virtue of their connexion with him, " the

Spirit of adoption," whereby they cry, " Abba, Father ; " that through Him they have " access with boldness and with confidence " to the throne of the heavenly grace, while they remain on earth ; and " rejoice in hope of the glory of God." If the blessings of the covenant which is sealed with the blood of Jesus, as of a Lamb without blemish and without spot, be—as well they may—so highly prized by his people, they should remember that IT IS A COVENANT which makes these high privileges sure to them, and that the same authority which secures the bestowment of the gifts, imposes upon the recipients of them peculiar and appropriate duties. We can neither have a divided covenant nor a divided Saviour. When the Redeemer with his salvation is truly received, his cause is taken " for better for worse, for richer for poorer ; " and the pulsations of sanctified joy which beat in the renewed heart, move the hand to work for its increase and prosperity. The requirements and obligations which the new covenant enjoins, are all precious to those who have a saving interest in it ; and are looked upon by them less as duties than as privileges. This is one of the tests by which the power and reality of faith is to be tried. If we belong to Christ, his cause belongs to us ; and all our Missionary purposes and efforts should be associated with this principle : nor, indeed, can they be suitably maintained unless it be duly recognised and received. The Saviour has a cause in the fields of Missionary labour, which is languishing for want of suitable assistance. The Wesleyan Methodists have taken an active part in originating and supporting it in various localities ; but that Society is acting on the defensive in some places, and is diminishing its exertions in others, at a time when vigorous and aggressive movements against antagonist powers are at all points imperatively required.

XX.

THE Wesleyan Methodists are, therefore, called upon to increase their " gifts and offerings," for Missionary purposes and objects, in order that " the kingdom of God " may be extended amongst men. With a view to the attainment of this end, it is sometimes recommended

to the subscribers to our Missions, that they should double
the present amount of their annual contributions to the
Missionary Fund. But it is submitted whether it would
not be "a more excellent way," to urge the members of
the Society to adopt as a general rule the principle of
increasing the amount of pecuniary aid which they have
been accustomed to afford,—leaving it with every subscriber to judge to what extent it will be right and proper
to carry it out in his case, after a careful review of individual ability, in connexion with the solemn interrogatory,
"How much owest thou to thy Lord?" Justice to man,
as well as to the cause of God, seems to recommend the
adoption of such a plan as this, in preference to the other;
because it is quite possible that there may be subscribers
who have not the means of increasing their annual offerings from one to two guineas, who could, and would, if
requested to do so, add five or ten shillings to their present contributions; and an increase to that extent, on the
part of many, would be of great importance to the institution. On the other hand, there is still a large number of
those who have the means to do much more than merely
double the amount of their present subscriptions to the
fund: and why should any rule be laid down that might,
even by implication, offer them an excuse for not doing
so? The actual condition of the world, and the present
state of the Society, demand that "he that has much
should give plenteously, and he that has little should do
his diligence gladly to give of that little." If the Christian
church has acted properly in taking up this cause at all,
and in maintaining it in any degree, is it not trifling—
nay, is it not worse than trifling—with the claims of God,
and with the wants and miseries of man, for the members
of the church to act otherwise? Surely, if we are right in
doing any thing, we are bound to do every thing we can
to make known the " excellence of the knowledge of
Christ Jesus our Lord " to a world that is yet, to a fearful
degree, ignorant of his name and character. Let it, then,
be the aim and endeavour of all, not merely to double the
present amount of subscriptions, but to secure to the
Society an increase of pecuniary aid proportioned to the

means of each of the donors, and to the magnitude of the object contemplated,—the salvation of all men.

The practice of paying to the Society by quarterly instalments the subscriptions which were formerly paid annually in one sum, has been introduced with much success into some places; and there can be no doubt that the general adoption of such an arrangement would be attended with many advantages. In the first place, it would render it easier for persons to augment their subscriptions, and to pay them in advance, than it would be for them to do so on the plan usually followed; inasmuch as to many of the best friends of the cause, it would be more convenient to pay the amount of their contributions at four different periods, than it would be for them to give the entire sum at any one time. This mode of payment would also extend the flow of the Society's income into the general fund more equally over the year, and would greatly diminish the necessity which now exists for borrowing money on interest, to meet the current expenditure. It should be remembered, that the disbursements for which a Missionary institution is required to provide, during the year, cannot be postponed or limited at any time, as those of the British and Foreign Bible Society, or any similar institution, may be, when it finds that it is conducting its operations on a scale which exceeds the rate of its income. These Societies can contract their issues at pleasure, and at once make arrangements for proportioning their appropriations to their receipts. The establishment which a Missionary institution has to maintain is a living one; and, whether contributions to the Wesleyan Missionary Society come in regularly or not, there are upwards of seven hundred Missionaries and subordinate agents, a large proportion of whom have families more or less depending upon the funds of that Institution for the means of subsistence from day to day, and whose drafts upon the General Treasurers have to be met by moneys borrowed on interest, whenever the remittances received from the Auxiliary and Branch Societies are insufficient for that purpose. It is, therefore, for obvious reasons, most desirable to devise such measures as may secure a regular and continuous income to the parent institution from the numerous sources in the country from which its revenue is derived. The punctual payment of subscriptions, whether weekly, monthly, or quarterly, to the Local Treasurers, and promptitude in the transmission of the amount to the General Treasurers, on the part of all the local officers, at least four times a year, would be an important step towards the introduction of an improved state of things in this respect; and while it would lessen the care and anxiety of those to whom the management of this great work is more especially intrusted, it would most certainly be attended with pecuniary advantages, by the saving which it would effect in the payment of interest. The separate sums forwarded on this plan might indeed be small, but the aggregate amount would be considerable; and these regular payments would be much increased, if, in every place throughout the kingdom, the friends of the Society were to connect with the praise-worthy exertions which they make to keep up and increase the Anniversary Collections, PAINS-TAKING endeavours, during the other periods of the year, to raise regular subscriptions. It is an unsafe thing to place too much dependence upon Anniversary Meetings and Anniversary Collections, because they are exposed to various contingencies, by which they may be, and often are, seriously affected.

XXI.

WITH suitable efforts to obtain additional aid from the present contributors to the Society, should be combined earnest and simultaneous exertions to increase the number of subscribers within the limits of every Auxiliary and Branch Society in the United Kingdom, and on all the foreign Stations. This may be attempted and accomplished in three ways: First, by persuading those who regularly attend our places of public worship,—whether fully united in church-fellowship with us, or hearers of the word only, who at present give towards the support of the Missions when public collections are made on their behalf,—to become subscribers for a certain specified amount. It will be found, on a careful examination of almost every congregation, that a number of individuals belonging to each of them give, from year to year, an uncertain sum at a Missionary Anniversary, who might, in addition to such service, assist the Society, by annual subscriptions; and who would, in all probability, do so, if the claims and necessities of the cause were properly placed before them, and their duty in relation to it pressed upon their attention in private personal interviews held with them for that purpose. How many persons have been induced to enter our communion, in consequence of " a word " of encouragement " spoken in season " to them by some zealous and watchful disciple, who had observed their regular and devout attendance on the ministry of the word! while some who are desirous of becoming members of the body, are prevented from taking this important step, because they have not been specifically invited. Subscribers to the Missions have not been sought for with sufficient care and diligence; and, in consequence of this neglect on our part, the number of names in the subscription-lists generally is much smaller than otherwise it would be. The influence of neighbourhood, of character, of station, and of domestic relations, have not been brought to bear sufficiently on this point; and it is high time that it should be so employed, as the effect of such a proceeding would be most favourable to the progress and prospects of the Missions. It has been justly observed by a distinguished friend of the Society in Lancashire, that there are perhaps none of the subscribers to its funds who might not, by a judicious application of personal influence, do more towards its support, than is done by the amount of direct pecuniary aid contributed by any one of them at the present time. Each subscriber should look around the social circle in which he moves, and should endeavour to induce at least another to unite with him in doing good in this particular way; remembering that influence is a talent for the proper use and application of which we are accountable to Him who shall hereafter " reward every man according to his works."

A second method by which the number of Missionary contributors may be very much enlarged is, by Christian

parents making the children under their care and direction subscribers to the Society; and that, not from mere
caprice, but on the ground of scriptural duty and obligation. By the sacrament of baptism, children are admitted into the church, and are dedicated to the service of
God. They are thus, at the request of their parents, who
act for them in this important matter, placed in new
relations, and are made the partakers of valuable privileges: for, while the doctrine of personal baptismal
regeneration is utterly rejected as unscriptural, and of
dangerous tendency, the sacrament itself should neither
be despised nor neglected. It is a Christian institution,
and is designed to lead to gracious ends and purposes,
intimately connected with the welfare of those to whom
it is administered. When a child is presented in faith
by the parents at the baptismal font, and the prayers of
the congregation on its behalf are sincerely and believ-
ingly offered, it may reasonably be supposed that God
will honour the due observance of his own ordinance, and
that his blessing will not be withheld from the parents or
their offspring on such an occasion. In this solemn
transaction between God and man, the child is formally
admitted into a state of membership with the church;
and obtains a peculiar interest in some of those privileges
which belong to the evangelical Zion, especially those
which are connected with united prayers and supplications, and of pastoral oversight and attention; and should
the child die, in a state of infancy, the parents are con-
soled under the painful bereavement by the additional
assurance which is afforded them in connexion with this
divine ordinance, that, though "absent from the body,"
their child is "present with the Lord;" not, indeed,
because of baptism; but by virtue of the covenant of
grace, of which that sacrament is one of the outward
and visible seals, and the Author of which hath said,
"Suffer the little children to come unto me, and forbid
them not; for of such is the kingdom of God." Surely,
on these and other grounds, "it is meet, right, and" the
"bounden duty" of parents,—when they come seeking
the good of their offspring, by desiring, that they may,

by baptism, be "received into the ark of Christ's church,"
—to contribute, in their name and behalf, towards the
support and spread of that church in the world.   To this
extent, Christian parents, most assuredly, are pledged to
act for their offspring, until they are competent to judge
for themselves.   As soon as that period arrives, children
should be impressively and affectionately reminded of
what was done for them while they were incapable of
understanding these things ; the privileges and obligations
of church-membership should be set before them, and
they should be urged and entreated to take upon them
the discharge of duties which had been performed by
others on their account, for the cause of that Saviour in
whose name they were blessed in their earliest infancy.
By such a course of proceeding, children would be trained
to Missionary service ; and an impression in its favour
would be made on their minds from their tender years,
which, by the divine blessing, would "grow with their
growth, and strengthen with their strength," and from
which they would themselves derive many advantages.
Should the principle involved in these remarks be practically carried out by the heads and guides of families
"professing godliness," the salutary effect of such a course
of conduct would be speedily felt in the domestic circle, and
in the improved tone of society, as well as on the income
of Missionary and other religious institutions.   The crude
and erroneous notions which are entertained on these subjects would be improved and corrected: much of the
money which is now given to children for their personal
use and gratification, and which is not unfrequently mis-
spent or wasted, would be cast into the treasury of the
Lord ; and the junior members of families in this way
would learn to acquire habits of discrimination, of reflec-
tion, and of self-denial, from which, in future years, they
would derive great advantage.   If this plan be fairly
tried, the next age will witness a large accession of contributors to the cause of Missions at home, and of candidates for Missionary work abroad ; and from generation
to generation the great work of human salvation will
proceed with a constantly-increasing rapidity, until "all

shall know the Lord from the least of them unto the greatest of them."

A third plan for obtaining an increase of regular subscribers, and one which, at this time, requires particular attention in almost every place, is, that of re-canvassing the towns and villages throughout the kingdom in which Societies and Associations auxiliary to the parent institution exist, or in which there is a Wesleyan-Methodist congregation. The income of not a few of the local Societies suffers from a want of systematic exertion, and active efforts; both of which would be greatly promoted by the arrangements that a vigorous and well-regulated canvass for additional subscribers would render indispensable. The success of this measure would be much assisted, by increasing the present number of Collectors, and by dividing each town into districts of such a size as would enable all the Collectors to perform their duty well, without requiring such an expenditure of time and strength as would render the discharge of it inconvenient, or impracticable, to any one who might be induced to engage in so good an undertaking. It has been found from experience, that a large district is seldom well visited by the Collector, and that those persons within its limits who can afford to give but little, and who generally need much attention and encouragement, are not called upon for their subscriptions with that frequency which their peculiar circumstances require; in consequence of which, their humble but useful contributions are very often entirely lost to the Society. By so arranging the districts into which any one town is divided as to make it comparatively easy for the Collectors to visit them once a week, this evil will be greatly lessened, if not entirely prevented. In commencing a new canvass, a call should be made at every house, not for the purpose of soliciting pecuniary aid in the first instance, but of distributing Missionary information; after which, the Collectors should apply for subscriptions, founded upon the evidence which the published documents afford of the excellence of the enterprise for which that assistance is solicited. When the canvass takes place, one of the members of the local

Committee should accompany each Collector to the
various houses which may be visited, and encourage him
by his presence, advice, and influence. "The heart
knoweth its own bitterness," is a saying, the force of
which is often felt by the self-denying Missionary Collector, after unsuccessful attempts to overcome ignorance,
indifference, covetousness, and sceptical enmity or contempt. They have often to struggle with severe difficulties, and should have corresponding encouragement
afforded them. Nor are the grounds of encouragement,
on which they may at all times take their stand, either
few or small. It is their high privilege to reflect, while
engaged in this work of mercy, that they are promoting
the cause of the Saviour;—that very cause for which he
lived, and suffered, and "became obedient unto death,
even the death of the cross;" for which martyrs have
bled; for which Missionaries have laboured and died;
for the success of which the universal church daily prays;
which engages the counsels, and calls forth the powers, of
heaven; in which angels would esteem it an honour to be
employed; and for the ultimate triumphs of which "the
Son" "ever liveth to make intercession," and all the
attributes of the uncreated Godhead stand pledged. Collectors should never despair of success. Let them go
forth in the spirit of prayerful dependence on that Being
to whose cause they are ministering, and in whose hands
are the hearts of all men; for he can and will make their
way to prosper before them.

XXII.

THE practical utility of the preceding suggestions
greatly depends upon the observance of methodical
arrangement, combined with activity and diligence by
local Committees, Officers, and Collectors. No system of
this description, however perfect in its structure, and in
its adaptation to the object which it is designed to secure,
will work itself. The Society possesses, in its various
Auxiliary and Branch Associations, most admirable machinery; and the chief desideratum now is, that it should
be kept in a state of vigorous and constant operation, by
the influence of willing minds and active hands, doing the

work of the Lord *for the sake of the Lord.* It is not
novelty in organization, but earnestness of purpose, and
energy of effort, that are now especially required; and the
inventive faculty should be employed, not in fanciful theo-
rizing, but in heartily adopting the best methods for the
more effectual working of every part of the system which
is already in motion, and by means of which so much
good has been accomplished. The services that have been
rendered to the parent institution by Auxiliary Societies,
their Treasurers, their Secretaries, their Committees, and,
last, but greatest of all, by their Collectors, are beyond all
praise; and attention is here directed to the importance
of order and diligence in connexion with all their proceedings, not so much for the purpose of stirring up their
minds by way of remembrance, as of showing, in a few
particulars, how both may be rendered subservient to the
end proposed. This may be done in connexion with the
Meetings of the respective Committees, the distribution of
Missionary intelligence, with the collecting of subscriptions, and with monetary receipts and remittances. Let
a monthly meeting of the local Committees be held at
least in each Circuit-town, at the close of the Missionary
prayer-meeting; and in order that punctuality of attendance may be secured, let the Meetings be duly published,
and made in reality—what they were intended to be—
occasions•for the transaction of Missionary business.
There is reason to fear, that, in some cases, these meetings are seldom held, except on the near approach of the
period fixed for holding the Missionary Anniversary.
One principal cause of this omission is, that it is taken for
granted, either that there is nothing to be done, or that
the work to be performed is trifling and unimportant.
But there is always something which requires the attention of a Missionary Committee; and nothing connected
with so great an undertaking should be considered small
or trifling. On these occasions the members of Committees should make themselves acquainted with the state of
Missionary feeling and effort in the Circuit, the Missionary affairs of which are intrusted to their care and direction :—the Collectors should be present, to pay to the

Treasurer the moneys which they may have obtained from their subscribers, as well as for the purpose of receiving advice, counsel, direction, and encouragement, to which their valuable services so well entitle them :—the "Notices" and other Missionary publications should be appropriated, and measures adopted for their speedy and extensive circulation ; for, if this be in any instance neglected, the Missionary cause will most assuredly decline. The prompt distribution of the intelligence contained in these documents in every place, is indispensably necessary to the growth and increase of the entire system. It is the fuel which, under God, is to feed the Missionary fire which He has kindled in the church. The parent Society speaks to the subscribers through the medium of its official publications, from month to month, in reply to the very proper question, " Why should we support the Missions ? " and to withhold them, or to distribute them irregularly, or after great intervals of time, inflicts a serious wrong upon the Society, as well as upon the contributors. To increase the interest and usefulness of the local meetings, after the ordinary business has been duly settled, it might be found advantageous to spend some time in conversation upon instructive and animating topics of a Missionary character, for mutual edification and encouragement. Measures should be adopted to secure a special meeting of each Committee at least once a quarter; at which time every member, and every Collector, should, if possible, be present. On that occasion each Collector's book should be audited, all the moneys received during the preceding quarter should be paid in, and forwarded, with the least possible delay, through the proper channel, to the Mission-House.

A growing desire is felt and expressed for rendering the District Missionary Committees more effective and influential than they generally are ; and, as one means towards this result, it has been recommended that a meeting of the members should be called on the day appointed for holding the District Anniversary ; at which time every Circuit in the District should, if possible, be represented by at least one person, and the inquiries contained in

the subjoined note should be put and carefully considered.*

XXIII.

OTHER measures of a public nature are employed in
different parts of the kingdom, for promoting the interests
of the Missions; which might be extended with advantage, because they are calculated to diffuse and to
strengthen those principles and feelings upon which this
enterprise is founded, and by which, under the blessing of
the Great Head of the church, it is to be sustained and
conducted to a triumphant issue. Allusion is here made
to the plan which is adopted in the smaller towns and
villages, connected with some Circuits, of having an
appropriate sermon preached on the Lord's day immediately preceding the Anniversary Meeting ; a practice
greatly to be commended, because the attention of the
hearers is, in this way, directed to the strong claims which
the Missions have upon them, and to their duties and
responsibilities in relation to the kingdom of the Messiah.
These topics are made the subject of personal meditation,
and of domestic converse, during the intervening period
between the delivery of the discourse, and the evening
selected for the Missionary Anniversary ; and the people,
in consequence of what they had heard on the Sabbath,
repair to the Meeting, better prepared to listen to the
facts and reasonings of the speakers, as well as to contribute towards the cause which they advocate.

A method of conducting Missionary prayer-meetings,
which has been adopted in numerous instances, has been
found to add so much to their utility and interest, as to
entitle it to special attention, and to general imitation
throughout the Connexion. The plan referred to,
involves a careful and judicious selection, by the officiat-
ing Minister, of those portions of the "Notices" for the
month which he may deem the most suitable and impressive for the occasion ;—the pointing out with brevity and
clearness the practical lessons which the "readings" may
be calculated to teach ;—a few remarks on the geographical position, the natural history, and the civil, social,

* See Note B, at the end of the volume.

and religious state of the countries to which the attention
of the people may have been directed by the Missionary
communications to which they had listened ;—and his so
conducting the devotional parts of the service, as to render
them edifying, lively, and influential ; copious, without
tedious prolixity ; and appropriate, without cold formality.
The subject contained in the " Notices " will, indeed, not
unfrequently suggest appropriate topics for prayer :—
proofs of the growing prosperity of Missions will naturally
call forth expressions of devout thanksgiving and praise :
—intelligence of the opposition which Missionaries may
have had to encounter, or of trials and privations through
which they may have been called to pass, will awaken
sympathy on their behalf, and lead to the offering-up of
prayers for them " to Him that is able to save : "—
accounts of the removal of Missionaries by death, or of
the temporary suspension of their labours by sickness and
disease, will lead to earnest supplications on behalf of the
near relatives of the men who may have fallen while
valiantly fighting in " the high places of the field," and of
the churches and congregations that, by such dispensations, have been bereaved of their beloved Pastors ; and
also for the recovery of the afflicted, and for the continued
preservation of the Ministers of our Zion in foreign and
inhospitable climes :—and information of promising openings for usefulness into which Missionaries, in consequence of the number of their engagements, cannot enter,
unless others be sent to their assistance, will produce
acknowledgments of past unfaithfulness to the interests of
the Redeemer ; gratitude for privileges enjoyed in the
possession of the means of grace and salvation at home ;
and the forming of purposes and resolutions, in the
strength of grace, to render more befitting services to this
department of the work of the Lord in future.   It is one
of the advantages of extemporaneous prayer, and one of
the strongest arguments in favour of the practice, that, by
such a method of devotion, our intercessions and thanksgivings can be so constructed as to adapt themselves to
existing circumstances of every description, whether connected with individuals or with families, with the church

or with the world. Missionary prayer-meetings afford excellent opportunities for making this adaptation apparent and profitable ; and they should, as much as possible, be rendered subservient to that as well as to other objects. The observance of this mode of regulating those valuable services, requires the employment of both time and thought. But, what of that ? Every thing belonging to the work of the sanctuary should be done in the best manner, by him who is appointed to officiate in any part of it ; and in this particular duty an ample and a present reward is reaped, in the pleasure with which the people anticipate the return of these meetings, in the improved attendance upon them which is witnessed, in the satisfaction which they afford, in the good which is accomplished at home, and in the service which is thus rendered to Missionaries and to Missions abroad.

XXIV.

WITH every other method which may be employed to provide for the maintenance of the existing establishments belonging to the Society, for the occupancy of new Stations and for an increase of Missionaries, there should be connected earnest, confiding, and unceasing prayer " to the God and Father of our Lord Jesus Christ, of whom the whole family in heaven and earth is named," for the stability, increase, and prosperity of this undertaking. Without the help which He alone can afford, Missionary plans and labours would lead to no spiritual and holy results ; but, under his sanction and blessing, they will flourish permanently and abundantly. The supplications and intercessions which are made on behalf of this department of the work of God should include—in addition to other topics—prayer for the preservation of the life and health of Missionaries and their families ; for the raising up of a native agency in connexion with every District and Station occupied by the Society ; for the communication of a larger measure of a Missionary spirit to the church, leading its members to sympathize with the Heathen, and to devise more liberal things in making provision for their relief; and for the general outpouring of the Holy Spirit, especially upon the Directors of the Society at home, and its various agents and establishments throughout the world; that wisdom may be given to their counsels, and efficiency to their endeavours, for the evangelization of all nations.

The sudden and (humanly speaking) premature removal of Missionaries by death from the posts of usefulness which they were occupying, is one of those mysterious dispensations of Divine Providence which not only perplex our reason, but stagger our faith. Yet how frequently do they occur, and spread a gloom over the churches! It is not the pecuniary loss which a Missionary Society sustains by such painful events, that produces symptoms of sorrow and almost of despondency on these occasions. That consideration, though one of much importance, is at those times felt to be the least. It is the loss of the peculiar qualifications of the deceased for the station which he occupied, of promising talents, of ardent zeal, of the fruit of years of preparation for Missionary service, of acquired experience and influence ; all of which are often lost to the Society by the death of a single Missionary. To speculate upon the cause or causes of these visitations would be an unprofitable employment; but it cannot be otherwise than beneficial to reflect seriously upon them, and to consider how far we have done our duty in praying for Missionaries, more especially for those who are placed in circumstances of great peril and danger, that they may " abide under the shadow of the Almighty," and there find a place of refuge from " the pestilence that walketh in darkness," and from " the destruction that wasteth at noon-day." No doubt, it sometimes is the case that the agents of the Society are called to their eternal reward at an early period, that they may be saved from the evil to come; while in other instances these strokes of the rod are applied in order that we may learn to " cease from man," who " is as grass," and trust in Him alone who is " the same yesterday, to-day, and for ever." It is, however, by no means improbable that these afflictions are sometimes designed to reprove and correct our practical unbelief in the special providence and gracious promises of Almighty God, and our omission of duty towards the men who jeopard their lives in defence of the Gospel. Who, of all the friends of Missions, think of and pray for Missionaries when on the deep, or in the wilderness, or amongst deceitful and bloody men, or in tropical regions, as much as their case demands? On reviewing this matter, who amongst us but must be prepared to say, " I ' have left undone' the thing ' which' I ' ought to have done?'" Who, in this respect, has done his duty to the Missionary of the cross? who is doing it now? And yet there never was a period when greater earnestness of intercession for the preservation of faithful labourers in the foreign field was more necessary, because, in consequence of the straitened circumstances of the Society, the Committee are unable to supply the vacancies which disease and death have recently produced in the Missionary host.

The importance of raising up a native ministry in those places to which the Society has conveyed the Gospel, by the instrumentality of men who went from this country for that purpose, is a subject which has engaged much anxious attention. It is not to be expected that the United Kingdom should supply all the heathen world with Missionaries; and if even this were practicable, it is neither desirable nor necessary. Wherever Christianity in its truth and spirituality is introduced, it is intended that it should make provision for its own diffusion; and facts connected with its history prove, beyond all successful contradiction, that in due time it invariably does so. This tendency may indeed in some places be checked for a season by temporary causes, as it has been in the West Indies by the effects of the state of slavery which so long existed there; but if prayer be addressed to that Being whose prerogative it is to select his own agents and instruments for the accomplishment of his own purposes, he will remove out of the way that which hindereth; and will call men to the sacred office in all the Missionary churches, who will preach in languages vernacular to the people and to themselves. A hopeful commencement has already been made towards this desirable state of things. The London Missionary Society is making arrangements for training Native Teachers at Calcutta, at Bangalore and other places in the East; and also in connexion with their Missions in the Southern Hemisphere, and in the West Indies. Many useful Assistant Native Missionaries and Teachers are connected with the Wesleyan Missions in different parts of the world; and some admirable specimens of this class of labourers have already visited this country, who, by their spirit and ministrations, have caused the " thanksgivings unto God" of many on their account. It will readily be supposed that these agents, however deep their piety, or ardent their zeal, will require careful instruction and training; for if in this country it is deemed necessary that candidates for our ministry should pass through a suitable course of study, with a view to their future usefulness in the church, how much more necessary must such preparatory training be in the case of a Mandingoe man, or a Kaffer, an American Indian, a Negro, or a New-Zealander! As " the harvest truly is great, and the labourers are few," in heathen lands, let us therefore " pray the Lord of the harvest" that he would raise up labourers; and connect with these petitions, prudent and well-digested methods for preparing them to become skilful and devoted workmen. If this be done, we shall speedily enter upon a new and more glorious era in the history of our Missions. It may be that He who afflicts his people for their profit, designs, by the pecuniary trials to which he has subjected the Missionary Societies, to press this subject more forcibly upon their attention, and to conduct them to the adoption of measures which will undoubtedly accelerate the progress of the Gospel.

In the present state of the Wesleyan Missionary Society, prayer without ceasing should be made for the increase, and further manifestation, on the part of its members and friends, of a spirit of deeper sympathy for the Heathen, and of more abundant liberality in providing for their instruction and salvation. Eighteen hundred years have revolved since the Son of God, standing upon our earth, commissioned his Apostles to go and " disciple all nations ;" yet still the sun rises and sets upon various countries, filled with proofs and emblems of idolatrous worship; whose present inhabitants are as ignorant of "the only true God, and of Jesus Christ whom" he hath "sent," as were the people who dwelt in them when the Apostles began to "preach repentance and remission of sins in" the "name" of Jesus "at Jerusalem." We speak of hundreds of millions of Pagans; but do we a¹so pause, and, in the light which Christianity supplies, endeavour to form an estimate of the destitution, the misery, and the danger of each individual in those vast masses of immortal beings travelling towards the same eternity to which we ourselves are hastening?—but, O! under what different circumstances, as it respects their knowledge of its nature, and the means and motives which we so richly enjoy to assist in making a suitable preparation for it! While we are directed to "believe in Him that justifieth the ungodly," and listen to words of invitation from the Saviour, saying to us, "Come unto me, all ye that labour and are heavy laden, and I will give you rest;" they, alas! vainly offer on unholy altars "the fruit of the body for the sin of the soul." While we are shown "a fountain opened in the house of David for sin and for uncleanness," they seek to silence the voice of conscience within them, and to destroy the power which sin exercises over them, by self-inflicted tortures. While we are taught to worship a Being possessing, in an infinite degree, every perfection that can claim our implicit trust, supreme affection, and steadfast obedience, they daily adore the objects which material nature affords, or, what is, if possible, worse, offer religious worship to deities, whose lives were stained with the worst crimes that can dishonour human nature: so that, by this method, they learn to invest vice with a divine character, and their very religion becomes one of the chief causes of their wickedness and misery. Yet, for the salvation of these countless multitudes, how little, comparatively, has been attempted or accomplished! although there is much cause for thankfulness to Almighty God, who has crowned with success the disproportionate efforts which have been made. There is a larger amount of spiritual and moral machinery at work,

every day, for the benefit of the metropolis of England, than
has yet been provided for the recovery of many millions
of human beings living in portions of the globe, compared
with which England is only a speck, and her whole population an unit. What an appeal does their sad condition
make to our most tender sympathies ! But no description of the state of the Heathen, however appalling, no
motives, however powerful, will, without a special influence from God himself, produce in the church that degree
of pity for them, or of effort to help them, to which their
necessities give them so strong a claim. For as no man
ever feels adequately on account of his personal guilt and
misery as a sinner, or seeks with proper earnestness for
deliverance from it, until the Spirit of God convinces him
of sin, and makes him alive to his danger as a child of
wrath ; so neither will the church ever feel or labour for
the " world " that " lieth in wickedness" as she ought, till
the same Spirit shall, by his powerful operations, convince
the collective body of the faithful of the world's sinfulness
and wretchedness. To this end his presence and agency
should be sought and invoked, in the petitions and requests which we present at the mercy-seat of heaven ;
and, when this cry shall ascend from the dwelling-places
of Christians, and from their solemn assemblies, then
shall the church " enlarge the place of her tent, and
stretch forth the curtains of her habitation."

Prayer should be offered up for the promised outpouring
of the Holy Spirit, with a special reference to the stability,
increase, and prosperity of this undertaking ; and for the
conversion of the world to the faith of our Lord and
Saviour Jesus Christ. The supreme importance of this
duty is demonstrated by the nature of the primary object
that Missionary Societies contemplate ; which is, the salvation of the soul from sin, and the restoration of fallen
man to the favour and image of God. Various terms and
forms of expression are employed in the New Testament
to describe this work, which strongly mark its importance,
and prove that it can be accomplished only by a Divine
Author. It is " a new creation ;" a spiritual resurrection ; and believers are described as being, in this respect,

"born, not of blood, nor of the will of the flesh, nor of the will of man, but of God;" as having "put on the new man which after God is created in knowledge, righteousness, and true holiness." "Without me ye can do nothing," is a declaration, that, as a memorial, should be always before the eyes of Missionaries, and of the conductors of Missionary Institutions; because it asserts a principle upon which all their operations must be founded, in order that they may be successful. If we, as a Society, feel strong in ourselves, or suppose that there is an innate energy to be relied on in the instruments we are employing, by which idolatry, superstition, and wickedness of every name will be subdued, without the power of the Spirit of God, He will, doubtless, in some effectual manner, convince us of our presumption, and withhold from us the honour of bearing any important part in gathering the nations to the fold of Christ. But if, in the midst of all our exertions, we cherish and manifest a spirit of prayerful dependence upon Him with whom is the residue of the Spirit, he will bless us more and more in our domestic and foreign operations; and will lead us into fields where we shall reap more abundant fruit.

As prayer for the supplies of the Spirit of Christ Jesus is so essential to Missionary success, it is of the utmost importance, that all who, from a desire for the increase of the Redeemer's kingdom in the earth, pray for the promised effusion of the Holy Ghost, should have just conceptions of the nature of the blessing which they seek, in order that they may "pray with the Spirit, and with the understanding also." Important as is the duty now under consideration, and frequently and forcibly as the performance of it is urged, in discourses from the pulpit, and in addresses from the platform, there is often combined with great earnestness in pleading for it, much vagueness of apprehension concerning it. While the necessity of prayer for the outpouring of the Holy Spirit upon all nations is at once admitted by every Christian, it is not always remembered, that if "we" would "have the petitions that we desire of Him" to whom we pray, we must "ask according to his will." The entire evidence of the sacred volume upon this particular subject, if duly weighed and considered, will lead to this conclusion,—that fervent prayer for the effusion of the Spirit of God upon any part of the heathen world, to be prevailing, must be united with equally sincere and earnest efforts to introduce into it the chosen instrument which the Spirit himself has prepared, as the medium through which he ordinarily communicates to men " the things that are freely given to " them " of God." That medium is " the word of truth," —the Gospel of the grace of God, and especially the ministry of that word by the living voice. It pleases God " by the foolishness of preaching to save them that believe ; " and though the blindness of the natural man perceives no wisdom in this arrangement, and his wickedness prompts him to reject and to contemn it, he who formed it always has honoured, and always will honour, his own institutions and ordinances. If the church would participate in the promises of God, she must walk in the order of God. The scriptural warrant by virtue of which the church prays for the gathering of all nations into her fold, cannot be dissociated from the solemn obligations under which, by the enactments and examples recorded in the New Testament, she is placed to convey the message of mercy and salvation to every human being.

When our Lord, shortly before his ascension, met the eleven Apostles " on a mountain in Galilee," he said unto them,—and through them to as many as he is pleased to call to the pastoral office,—" Go ye therefore and teach all nations, baptizing them in the name of the Father, and of the Son, and of the Holy Ghost : teaching them to observe all things whatsoever I have commanded you : and, lo, I am with you alway, even unto the end of the world." Such is the commission given to the ministers of Christ. They are to go forth, " preaching the word," that men may be converted to the faith, initiated by baptism into the church, and be trained in the earthly sanctuary for the enjoyments and employments of the heavenly. To this end, the promise of the presence and co-operation of the Spirit of Christ with them is given for their encouragement and support. " Lo, I am WITH YOU alway,"—

to succeed your labours,—to enlighten, pardon, sanctify, and save them that " believe on me through " your " word ;" " and I am with you, even unto the end of the world," or of the present state.

The Acts of the Apostles confirm and illustrate the principle here laid down, as in the case of Cornelius, and in the circumstances connected with the introduction of the Gospel into Europe by St. Paul. That the " devout Centurion of the Italian band " might be made a partaker of the great salvation, the Apostle Peter was supernaturally directed to proceed from Joppa to Cæsarea, " to preach peace by Jesus Christ " to that officer and to his household ; and while St. Paul sojourned at Troas, on the shore of the Ægean Sea, he was summoned in a vision to cross over to Europe, in order that the work of salvation might be commenced there by his instrumentality. Such has been the divine method from the beginning until now ; nor have we any reason to expect that it will be altered, and least of all should we expect that it will be changed, for the purpose of affording encouragement to indifference or to indolence on the part of professing Christians. The Spirit of God accompanies the ministration of the truth of God ; and, therefore, the truth must first be exhibited, in order that men may be turned unto the Lord. One hundred and fifty years ago, prayers were offered in the churches of this land, that it might " please " God " to have mercy upon all men," and that his " way might be known upon earth ; " but little or nothing was then attempted for securing the accomplishment of the petitions which were offered ; and every thing, therefore, connected with true religion presented a gloomy and discouraging aspect. When the churches were awakened to a sense of their duty, and manifested a degree of activity in seeking to save mankind by sending forth the Gospel, the world displayed a measure of anxiety for the introduction of a better state of things than it had before known ; and in proportion as the activity of Christians has increased, the solicitude of the Heathen has been extended and deepened. Wherever the church has, in modern times, sent her messengers

into pagan nations to preach the Gospel, signs of
improvement are exhibited; but where they are not
found, the "sorrows" of the people are daily "multiplied." In some groups of islands in the Pacific Ocean,
idolatry is abolished; Christian temples are erected; the
ordinances of religion are established; knowledge is
spreading; useful arts are cultivated; laws, founded on
scriptural principles, are promulgated by the ruler, and
obeyed by the people; and all the elements of real
improvement are in operation: while in other groups,
at no great distance, the inhabitants have not emerged in
the smallest degree from their original state of ignorance
and misery. The cause of this disparity is obvious. It
is to be ascribed to the Gospel. If it had not been introduced amongst the inhabitants of the former, the church
would have prayed in vain for their salvation; and until
it shall be sent to them that dwell in the latter, they will
remain as they are, or rather they will grow worse and
worse, however constantly the church may pray for their
salvation. It is not intended, by these observations, to
limit the gracious operations of God, or to argue that they
are confined within the circle in which the appointed
means of grace are enjoyed; but to expose the incon-
sistency of talking of and praying for the outpouring of
the Holy Spirit upon the world, without corresponding
endeavours to extend the knowledge of the Gospel of
salvation. What God in his sovereignty may do, is one
thing; what he has made it our duty to do, is another.
It is not because God has forgotten his promise, that so
many millions of our species are ignorant of him; but
because the church was for so long a period inattentive to
her obligations and responsibilities. These things are
now better understood. A nobler spirit—"the spirit of
love, of power. and of a sound mind"—is manifesting
itself in relation to the cause of Missions; and the inquiry
is becoming more and more general, "How shall" the
Heathen " call on Him in whom they have not believed?
and how shall they believe in Him of whom they have
not heard? and how shall they hear without a preacher?
and how shall they preach, except they be sent?"

XXV.

THESE are the claims which, at the present crisis, the Wesleyan Missionary Society presents : a prompt and cordial compliance with which, on the part of all those to whom they are more especially addressed, would effectually extricate this Christian Institution from all the pecuniary difficulties that are so severely felt ; and, what is even still more important, would bring down upon all the agents and agencies placed under its direction a larger measure of " the heavenly gift of the Holy Ghost."

The duties which have been pointed out are all reasonable, as well as practicable ; and are not only clothed with the authority of the Divine Lawgiver, but are also enforced upon us by the power of divine examples. We are taught, by the processes of sacrifice and of suffering which were connected with the great work of our Redemption by Christ Jesus, that the principle to be adopted and acted upon by every Christian, in his endeavours to promote the final cause for which these sacrifices and sufferings were made and endured, is, that THE LIMIT OF INDIVIDUAL ABILITY IS THE ONLY LIMIT OF INDIVIDUAL DUTY AND OBLIGATION. " God so loved the world, that he gave his only-begotten Son, that whosoever believeth in him should not perish, but have everlasting life." The infinite resources of the Godhead could provide no greater gift, the exigencies of the case could be met by nothing less. The world, " dead in trespasses and sins," could be made to live only through and by the death of the only-begotten Son ; or that Son—who is " the brightness of the Father's glory, and the express image of his person," and who, as such, is the object of his infinite and eternal regard and affection—would have been " spared," instead of having been " delivered up for us all." An emergency had arisen immediately connected with man, but affecting in various ways the entire intelligent creation of God, which, for reasons too profound to be fathomed by any creature, however exalted, required the utmost to be done to meet it that boundless wisdom, power, and love could devise and effect ; and THAT UTMOST WAS DONE.

" The ransom was paid down, the fund of heaven—
Heaven's inexhaustible, exhausted fund —
(Amazing and amazed) pour'd forth its price,
All price beyond."

For " when the fulness of the time was come, God sent
forth his Son made of a woman, made under the law,
to redeem them that were under the law, (and under
the curse,) that we might receive the adoption of children." The Son of God voluntarily participated in this
transaction. The cross was not forced upon him: he
took it up; and, for "the joy that was set before him,"—
joy springing from the contemplation of the recovery of
all nations to his fold,—he " endured the cross, despising
the shame." WHAT COULD HE DO MORE THAN GIVE
HIMSELF, and, " WHILE WE WERE YET SINNERS," DIE
" FOR US?" The principle which is here contended for,
still regulates the arrangements and movements of heavenly powers in heavenly places, in relation to the recovery of the world to holiness and to God. As " the
Head" of the body " the church," all things are placed
under the dominion of the King Messiah. He is set
" far above all principality, and power, and might, and
dominion, and every name that is named, not only in this
world, but also in that which is to come; " and all beings,
(He only excepted who hath set Him at his own right
hand,) all powers, all agencies, every thing material and
spiritual, great and small, simple and complex, above,
around, and beneath, are placed under him, that he may
" subdue all things unto himself," and thus finish the mystery of the wisdom and goodness of God towards our race.

If, then, the narratives of the Evangelists are not fabu-
lous; if there were truth and reality in the delightful
spectacle which the shepherds beheld in the manger at
Bethlehem—in the amazing occurrences in the wilderness, whither Jesus was led to be tempted of the devil—
in the scenes of humiliation and agony which were witnessed in the garden of Gethsemane, and on the hill of
Calvary—in the exaltation of Jesus to be a Prince and a
Saviour;—if these things actually took place, then the
manifestation of " the Word" that " was God" in an

infant's form—the endurance of Satanic temptation by the
Son of God, that he might know how to succour them
that are tempted—the groans and tears, the mental
anguish and accursed death, of the innocent Victim—the
energy and earnestness with which he is carrying out his
saving designs and purposes—proclaim, in language the
most unequivocal and powerful, to all his people, that, IN
WORKING TOGETHER WITH HIM, FOR THE SALVATION OF
THE WORLD, THE LIMIT OF THEIR ABILITY IS THE ONLY
LIMIT OF THEIR DUTY AND OBLIGATION IN SERVING
HIM. The conclusion is clear and irresistible : " Beloved,
if God so loved us, then ought we," according to our
means and opportunities, " so to love one another." Increased privileges bring with them increased duties and
obligations. If we live in days which kings and prophets
desired to behold, and partake of the blessedness of the
higher dispensation under which we are placed, we must
be prepared to yield a more extensive and self-denying
obedience. Christ " came not to destroy the law and the
prophets," but to carry out the principles involved in
them. He did not come to diminish the obligations of
the law, by which the offerings of the Jews were regulated, to whom the mercy-seat was covered with a typical
veil; but that, by disclosing to us, in his doctrine and in
his death, the matchless love of God, the sphere of our
pious and benevolent exertions might be extended to the
uttermost. Christianity must be taken with its peculiar
duties, as well as with its peculiar advantages. Both are
identified with the cross. Gifts and offerings to the glory
of God, and for the benefit of man, are to be regulated by
that standard. It is the rule of duty in this great cause,
as well as the object of faith. The love which induced
the Saviour to bleed on the cross, when " shed abroad " in
the human "heart," supersedes Mosaic statutes ; and the
services which Christianity requires are left to be determined by the full and generous operation of Christian
principle, abiding in the believer. It is as useless and
dangerous to go to Sinai to ascertain the limit of evangelical obedience, as it would be to go there to ascertain
the extent of evangelical salvation.

Neither the one nor the other of these can be accurately traced amidst the blackness and darkness which was intermingled with the fire upon the Mount; and should, therefore, be viewed through some more fitting medium. If we would be men in experience and in practice in these " deep things of God," we must repair to that " one place" in Jerusalem, in which the disciples met " with one accord," and read their meaning in the light radiating from the lambent flames which rested on the heads of the chosen Apostles on the day of Pentecost. So deeply did the converts who were made on that memorable day, feel the truth and importance of the principle pleaded for in this section, that they passed at once from Mount Horeb to Mount Zion, in reference to obedience as well as privilege, and stretched their liberality, beyond positive legal requirements, to an extent commensurate with the new and expansive feeling of which they had been made the happy partakers ; for they " sold their possessions and goods, and parted them to all men, as every man had need." That was the spirit which lived and flourished in primitive Christianity ; and such was one of the lovely fruits which it produced. This spirit was nobly exemplified by the great Apostle of the Gentiles, in the generous sentiments which he uttered, and in the self-denying and laborious services which he endeavoured to render to all classes of men, in every place that he visited. Convinced that the interests of the Gospel required him to proceed from Ephesus to Jerusalem, he repaired to the latter city at great risk and hazard to himself. The power of friendship, sanctified and strengthened by religion,—the influence of Christian associations and ties of the most endearing character,—the prospect of martyrdom,—were insufficient to shake his purpose, or to deter him from acting in accordance with the sentiment,—*that the only limit of our duty in the service of the Redeemer, is the limit of our ability.* Hence, in reply to tears and remonstrances, and alarming predictions, he said, " What mean ye to weep and to break mine heart? for I am ready not to be bound only, but also to die at Jerusalem for the name of the Lord Jesus." St. Paul was no rash enthusiast. He never

wantonly exposed his life. He was restrained from it by
the very sense of duty to the Lord which led him to go
up to Jerusalem, with his life in his hand, on that memorable occasion. The Master called him, and he immediately prepared to obey the summons. His compliance
might lead him into a prison, or to death ; but " none of
these things moved him, neither counted he his life dear
unto himself, so that he might finish his course with joy,
and the ministry which he had received of the Lord
Jesus, to testify the Gospel of the grace of God." The
principle upon which he himself acted, he laid down as
the standard to which he urged others to conform in the
performance of Christian duty. In the appeal which he
addressed to the Corinthian converts, on behalf of their
impoverished brethren in Palestine, he fixed their attention chiefly upon the manger and the cross, and pressed
the practical love of their neighbour upon them by
motives which only the love of the Saviour towards them,
and towards all men, can supply; and which, indeed,
when properly understood and felt, render all others
unnecessary. " For ye know the grace of our Lord Jesus
Christ, that, though he was rich, yet for your sakes he
became poor, that ye through his poverty might be rich."
That was the sublime example which he set before them,
and which all the followers of the Saviour are to exert
themselves to imitate at all suitable opportunities. Jesus
emptied himself, that we might be filled. He assumed a
state of poverty, that we might be enriched. He " took
upon him the form of a servant," that we might again
become the " sons and daughters" of " the Lord God
Almighty." He " humbled himself," that we might be
exalted ; and endured death under its most appalling and
revolting forms, that we might attain everlasting life and
blessedness. Though the disciple cannot stoop and suffer
as the Master did, the same spirit of sacrifice which was
displayed by Him on our behalf, should animate his
followers in their endeavours to extend his dominion,
and to gain for him the love and the obedience of the
whole human family. Men who really deserve the name
of " Missionaries of the cross," participate largely of this

disposition. "For his name's sake" they go forth to labour in distant lands. "For his name's sake" they breathe the tainted air which pervades the western coast of Africa; they climb the mountains and ascend the rivers of the southern extremity of that continent; they dwell amongst cannibals in the islands of the Pacific; they penetrate the remote wilderness, and, in its deepest recesses, seek the souls for whom the Saviour died. Feelings of patriotism, the strength of filial and fraternal love, all personal interests and considerations, are brought into subjection to this self-denying and self-annihilating spirit. It is not to be supposed that this is possessed in an equal degree by every Missionary; but it should be well understood by every one who aspires to the office of a Missionary to the Heathen, that, whatever may be his other qualifications for this service, no man is fit for it who is not resolved, in the strength of grace, to take up and practically to carry out the principle upon which these observations are founded. For if he love even father or mother, or sister or brother, or houses or lands, more than this part of the work of the Saviour, he is not worthy to be engaged in it. The same spirit should govern every Pastor and member of the church at home, in devising plans, and in furnishing contributions, for the furtherance of Missionary objects. We are not to deal out our gifts as if we were bestowing an alms, or performing a distasteful duty and service. It was not thus that the Saviour acted towards us. The manifestations of his pity were not forced from him as wine from the grapes, but flowed forth spontaneously, as water from the gushing fountain. What He only could do for our race, that he did; and what we can do for his cause, we should do cheerfully and liberally, and as if we felt it to be a privilege to be permitted to minister to its growth and increase in the world. The duties to which the churches are thus called at the present Missionary crisis, are of great magnitude and difficulty; and when we compare the feeble exertions which we have individually made, with the extent of our duty and obligation, we may well exclaim, "Enter not into judgment with thy servants, O Lord!" At the same time, it is cheering to reflect, that there have been instances of moral heroism on the part of Missionaries, and proofs of liberality on the part of private Christians, connected with modern Missions, which are worthy of the first and purest ages of Christianity. Yet it is deeply to be regretted, that the receipts of the Wesleyan Missionary Society have, during four or five successive years, fallen short of the amount which it has so frequently and so solemnly declared to be necessary to meet the exigencies of the world. It is indeed a cause of hope and thanksgiving, that the Income for the year 1841 exceeded the expenditure for the same period; but, amidst our rejoicings on this account, let it not be forgotten, that if the Society had kept up its amount of agency to the extent necessary for the vigorous prosecution of the work of God amongst the perishing millions of idolaters who are ignorant of his name and character, the debt of the Society would have been further increased. This would have been the case, if even the vacancies occasioned by death, and by the return of Missionaries on account of the failure of health, had been adequately supplied; and if reasonable expectations of assistance, in places where the want of it is most painfully and injuriously felt, had been fulfilled. The fruit of the exertions of the last year, especially when the state of all the great interests of the country is taken into consideration, is most honourable and most cheering. It teaches us what, by the divine blessing, may accomplished; and will encourage us to increase our exertions. The Committee must expend much more in the course of the current year, than they ventured to do during the last; and the members and friends of the Society must prepare for these arrangements, or otherwise they will grieve the hearts of all their Missionaries; they will destroy the health of some of them; and shorten the lives of others by excessive labour, who went out relying upon the pledges of generous and steady sympathy and support which were given to them; they will restrain the tide of mercy that is ready to flow over regions long parched and desolate; and avert from themselves, and from others around them, the blessings promised when "all the tithes

are brought into the Lord's storehouse." If every one
does according to the ability which God hath given him,
all that is required will be accomplished by united, continuous, and prayerful efforts; and no individual will be
unduly burdened. Various plans have been recommended
to the Society for relieving it from pecuniary difficulties;
and though the persons with whom they have originated
differ in the opinions which they entertain as to the best
mode for the accomplishment of that object, they all
agree, that it is not merely practicable, but will be found
a comparatively easy task, to liquidate the debt due by
the Society, and so to augment the Income as to enable
the Treasurers to meet the claims which are made upon
them.   And so it will be found, if the attempt be made
on the great rule and motive which Christianity pre-
scribes : " Freely ye have received, freely give." Let us
aim at this, as a means in order to the attainment of the
end which we have in view,—the increase and completion
of that spiritual temple which God is rearing out of the
ruins of human nature, by the operation of the word of
truth, and the Spirit of righteousness, and on whose front
shall be inscribed : " The kingdoms of this world are
become the kingdoms of our Lord, and of his Christ; and
He shall reign for ever and ever ! " While too many professing Christians are contending for modes and forms of
religious worship, it is especially the calling, as it has
been, during the last hundred years, the avowed object, of
the Wesleyan Methodists, to endeavour to disseminate, as
extensively as possible, the great principles of scriptural
Christianity, leaving them to assume such forms as, under
the divine blessing, may render them most conducive to
the glory of God, and to the salvation of mankind. Compared with " the excellency of the knowledge of Christ
Jesus the Lord," that which is circumstantial and ceremo-
nial is but as the chaff to the wheat : and " what is the
chaff to the wheat ? saith the Lord." Here is the true
remedy for all the evils that afflict the world ; and here is
the world's hope. While the waters of political and social
strife and agitation disturb the nations, and threaten them
with destruction, the Gospel is seen by the eye of faith as

God's " faithful witness in heaven," affording a pledge and
an earnest of that bright and lovely period, when the
floods of human passion shall no longer lift up their voice,
when the pacific influence of the heavenly Dove shall per-
vade the mind and the heart of the world, and when " the
work of righteousness shall be peace, and the effect ot
righteousness, quietness and assurance for ever." Temporary reverses may occur to try our faith, and to check
our presumption ; but ultimate failure is impossible. The
morning of the day of the millennial glory of the church
is breaking upon the mountains ; and the evangelical sun
shall shine more and more, until it clothe both hemispheres at once with beauty and with glory. Nothing can
stand before the church, when she learns her obligations,
and draws her motives, from the cross. Then every section of the church, and every Minister and member
belonging to each, shall esteem and love every thing less
than the Redeemer and his service. Then " prayer shall
be made for Him continually, and daily shall He be
praised." Intellect, learning, life, health, and property
will be laid upon his altar. No one will then be found
praying for the coming of the kingdom of Christ, without
adding to his prayers suitable endeavours to secure the
fulfilment of his petition. The " messengers of the
churches " will be multiplied. Missionaries will joyfully
live and die for Christ's sake in foreign lands ; and it will
be their choice to occupy a grave in those countries in
which their spiritual descendants shall dwell, rather than
have a resting-place assigned to them amongst the tombs
of their ancestors. Contributions for the conversion of
the world shall be increased and multiplied. All the
talent, and zeal, and influence of Missionary Committees
and Collectors will be brought to bear on Missionary
interests ; and supplications will be constantly offered for
the descent of the Holy Ghost upon all the earth. The
church having thus come up to the point of obedient
faith, by acting to her utmost ability for the glory of God,
and the salvation of the world, He with whom " is the
residue of the Spirit " will magnify his " word " of promise
" above all " his " name ; " and " a nation shall be born in

a day." Then he will put forth the saving strength of his right hand, and, throwing open the prison-doors of the captives of hope, will bid them go forth, and turn to the strong-holds prepared for them.

We have embarked in a great enterprise, and have corresponding encouragement afforded us. We have promises such as God alone has authority to give : " As thy days, so shall thy strength be." We have assistance such as God only can bestow: " My grace is sufficient for thee : for my strength is made perfect in weakness." We have examples such as the word of God alone can furnish : " In nothing I shall be ashamed, but that with all boldness, as always, so now also Christ shall be magnified in my body, whether it be by life, or by death. For to me to live is Christ." We have rewards such as God only can confer : Rewards too great for men to receive in all their fulness on earth, but which shall be distributed at the resurrection of the just, when "they that be wise shall shine as the brightness of the firmament, and they that turn many to righteousness, as the stars for ever and ever." Unfurl, then, in every clime that banner under which the church is always victorious. Let the message of mercy be sent into all the earth, that the fainting spirit of man may be revived. Cry aloud, and spare not, that the nations may shout for joy. Then the church shall see, and flow together, and her heart shall fear and be enlarged. Her sun shall no more go down, neither shall her moon withdraw itself; for the Lord shall be her everlasting light, and the days of her mourning shall be ended. What his word of promise has declared, that his word of power will accomplish ; and he " will glorify the house of his glory." " The mountain of" his " house shall be established on the tops of the mountains, and shall be exalted above the hills, and all nations shall flow unto it." The ensign of salvation shall wave in every breeze, shall be seen by every eye, and shall be hailed by every tongue, with joyful acclamations. Great expectations these ! Yes, but they rest on a glorious basis,—a basis formed of divine promises, oaths, and blood. " The arm of the Lord shall be made bare in the eyes of all nations, and all flesh

shall see the salvation of God." "I have sworn by myself, saith the Lord, the word is gone out of my mouth in
righteousness, and shall not return, that unto me every
knee shall bow, every tongue shall swear." "And they
sung a new song, saying, Thou art worthy to take the
book, and to open the seals thereof; for thou wast slain,
and hast redeemed us to God by thy blood, out of every
kindred, and tongue, and people, and nation." "WORTHY
IS THE LAMB THAT WAS SLAIN TO RECEIVE POWER,
AND RICHES, AND WISDOM, AND STRENGTH, AND HONOUR,
AND GLORY, AND BLESSING. And every creature which
is in heaven, and on the earth, and under the earth, and
such as are in the sea, and all that are in them, heard I
saying, BLESSING, AND HONOUR, AND GLORY, AND POWER,
BE UNTO HIM THAT SITTETH UPON THE THRONE, AND
UNTO THE LAMB FOR EVER AND EVER."

NOTES.

NOTE A.—Page 2.

THE subjoined List is extracted from the "American Almanack, and
Repository of Useful Knowledge," which is generally reckoned a competent authority on this subject.

TABULAR VIEW OF THE RELIGIOUS DENOMINATIONS IN THE UNITED
STATES.

Denominations.	Churches or Congregations.	Ministers.	Members or Communicants.
Baptists	6,319	4,239	452,000
Ditto, Freewill	753	612	33,876
Ditto, Seventh-Day	42	46	4,503
Ditto, Six-Principle	16	10	2,117
Catholics	418	478	
Chrystians	1,000	800	150,000
Congregationalists	1,300	1,150	160,000
Dutch Reformed	197	192	22,515
Episcopalians *	950	849	
Friends	500		
German Reformed	600	180	30,000
Jews			
Lutherans	750	267	62,266
Mennonites	200		30,000

* A branch of the Church of England.

Denominations.	Churches or Congregations.	Ministers.	Members or Communicants.
METHODISTS (Wesleyans) *		3,106	686,549
Moravians, or United Brethren	24	33	5,745
Mormonites			12,000
New-Jerusalem Church	27	33	
Presbyterians....................	2,807	2,225	274,084
Ditto, Cumberland..............	500	450	50,000
Ditto, Associate	183	87	16,000
Ditto, Reformed	40	20	3,000
Ditto, Associate Reformed	214	116	12,000
Shakers	15	45	6,000
Tunkers	40	40	3,000
Unitarians	200	174	
Universalists	653	317	

NOTE B.—Page 79.

INQUIRIES.

1. HAVE you a regularly organized Committee, Treasurer, and Secretary?

2. How often does the Committee meet?

3. Is the town regularly divided into such a number of Collecting Districts, as render the thorough canvassing of the town a task of easy accomplishment?

4. What number of Collectors are employed?

5. How many more are necessary?

6. Do they call at every house?

7. Do they call punctually on the weekly, monthly, and quarterly Subscribers when their respective Subscriptions are due, and not call for two or three Subscriptions at once?

8. Are the Missionary Prayer-Meetings kept up, and rendered interesting?

9. Is care taken to diffuse Missionary information by the prompt distribution of the Missionary publications?

10. What number of preaching-places in the Circuit?

11. The number in Society and Congregation?

12. Whether Missionary Meetings at all? and, if not, public collections?

13. Whether Collectors at every place?

* Their social importance and respectability are well known in America. Some of the highest offices in the country are filled by Methodists

CONTENTS.

CONTENTS.

THE END.

LONDON :—PRINTED BY JAMES NICHOLS, HOXTON-SQUARE.

www.ingramcontent.com/pod-product-compliance
Lightning Source LLC
Chambersburg PA
CBHW021202020426
42331CB00003B/168